Vanguard of Expansion

Army Engineers in the Trans-Mississippi West

1819–1879

by

Frank N. Schubert

Historical Division
Office of Administrative Services
Office of the Chief of Engineers

Fredonia Books
Amsterdam, The Netherlands

Vanguard of Expansion:
Army Engineers in the Trans-Mississippi West
1819-1879

by
Frank N. Schubert

ISBN: 1-58963-606-6

Reprinted from the 1980 edition

Fredonia Books
Amsterdam, the Netherlands
http://www.fredoniabooks.com

Foreword

Americans have always shown a special interest and pride in the heritage of the frontier. The popular culture abounds in celebrations of cowboys and cavalrymen, pioneers and prospectors. Behind these heroes were others, Army Engineers who surveyed roads, laid out forts that protected them, and made the maps that guided travelers over them. Generally unsung and little known outside a small group of scholars and buffs, these officers provided indispensable services to a growing nation.

In *Vanguard of Expansion,* Dr. Schubert has told the story of the many contributions of the Engineers in the cause of westward expansion. His concise narrative should be of interest to all who are fascinated by the epic tale of America's march to the Pacific.

J. W. Morris
Lieutenant General, USA
Chief of Engineers

The Author

Frank N. Schubert, the author of several articles on the frontier Army, is an historian with the Historical Division, Office of the Chief of Engineers. He holds a Ph.D. degree from the University of Toledo.

Preface

This book contains a compact narrative of Corps of Engineers activities in the trans-Mississippi West during the years of expansion and settlement. The work of the Corps in the West encompassed a wide range of services, from basic exploration and cartography to road surveys and the first river and harbor improvements on the Pacific coast. Through the entire period, in all their diverse assignments, Corps officers worked to bind this huge new country to the old, to increase the public's understanding of the West, and to develop critical networks of communication and transportation.

This study is not a definitive treatment of the subject. William H. Goetzmann's fine book, *Army Exploration in the American West, 1803-1863*, can more justly claim such a distinction. Yet, while Goetzmann's book is comprehensive, it is also massive. This publication seeks to reduce to a more convenient size the story of the diverse contributions of the Corps to Western development. For readers both inside and out of the Corps of Engineers, we hope this narrative will provide an adequate overview of a complex and fascinating subject.

Numerous people contributed to the production of this narrative and helped it become better than it otherwise would have been. An historian's best friend is a capable reference librarian, and this writer's best friend is Irene Schubert, a superb librarian and head of the reference department at the University of Maryland Undergraduate Library. Throughout the research and writing she answered numerous queries on diverse subjects willingly and well. Others who were more than ordinarily helpful were Joan Hoffman, Yale University Libraries; James Corsaro, New York State Library; Gary L. Morgan, Cartographic Archives Division, National Archives; William A. Deiss, Smithsonian Institution Archives; and Ann P. Crumpler, U.S. Army Corps of Engineers Library. Here at the Historical Division, numerous colleagues—both past and present—read and criticized the manuscript in various stages of development. Among those who provided useful commentaries and other assistance were Alfred M. Beck, Margaret B. Combs, Albert E. Cowdrey, Lenore Fine, John T. Greenwood, Agnes M. Riedel, and Paul K. Walker. Robert W. Coakley and William G. Bell of the U.S. Army Center of Military History also made helpful suggestions, as did Clifford Nelson of the United States Geological Survey and Jerry W. Crenshaw of the Office of Administrative Services, Office of the Chief of Engineers. Stephanie Demma edited the manuscript, which was typed by Ruth E. Steers and Earline H. Lomax. For interpretations made, conclusions drawn, and any errors of omission or commission, the author alone is responsible.

Table of Contents

Introduction

Even before the United States won its independence from Great Britain, westward expansion was a powerful force among Americans. So strong was the compulsion to seek the new country that the British, fearing loss of control over migrating colonists and war with the Indians, tried to halt the westward movement by decree. The Royal Proclamation of 1763 was predictably unsuccessful. By the time of the Revolution, the westering urge was firmly imbedded in American society.

The newly independent United States offered ample space for its mobile, restless citizens. Bordered by Spanish Florida to the south and British Canada to the north, the nation stretched from the Atlantic Ocean to the Mississippi River. Most settlements were still east of the fall line on the slopes of the Appalachian Mountains. Far from being trackless wilderness, the scantily populated woodlands and river valleys of the interior were laced with trails that linked the yet unconquered native peoples. But to the Anglo-Americans, trans-Appalachia was imperfectly known and indifferently charted.

While pioneers poled flat-bottomed boats down the Ohio River and led oxcarts through the Cumberland Gap, President Thomas Jefferson added another huge domain to the nation. The purchase of Louisianna grew out of Jefferson's desire to obtain the port of New Orleans from France. When the French government expressed its willingness to part with all of Louisiana, Jefferson leaped at the opportunity. The vaguely defined territory, which stretched north and west from New Orleans to Canada and the Rocky Mountains, was fully as large as the United States itself.

Even before completing the negotiations, Jefferson intended to send an exploring party across the Mississippi to the Rockies and beyond, "even to the Western Ocean." The government lacked an agency to administer such an enterprise, a depot for maps and instruments, and a pool of trained explorers versed in surveying, cartography, and topographical drawing. Consequently, Jefferson had to create his expedition out of whole cloth, down to assembling such maps and information on the vast region as then existed. Captain Meriwether Lewis, Jefferson's choice to command the party, underwent an intensive education in scientific observation and collection at the American Philosophical Society's Philadelphia headquarters before setting off with Captain William Clark and a small band of frontiersmen.[1] Their successful journey of 1804-1806, up the Missouri River and over the mountains with the intrepid

Sacajawea as a guide, then down the Columbia River to the Pacific Ocean, was all the more remarkable for their scant training and experience.

Four more expeditions departed for portions of Louisiana during Jefferson's presidency. In 1804 William Hunter and John Dunbar made an abortive attempt to follow the Red River to its source in Spanish Texas, and a year later Spanish soldiers thwarted a similar effort by Thomas Freeman. Lieutenant Zebulon M. Pike ranged far over the new country on explorations of 1805-1806 and 1806-1807. Although he erroneously claimed to have found the source of the Mississippi, he did explore much of the river's upper reaches. On his second journey, he also examined large parts of the Southwest before Spanish forces arrested him and confiscated his papers. Pike won wide acclaim for his exploits, and indeed his efforts were far more significant than those of either Hunter and Dunbar or Freeman.[2]

All of Jeffersonian expeditions shared important characteristics. Their commanders, although men of intelligence and courage, were novice explorers. Some possessed frontier experience, but none were trained specifically for exploration. Pike, for example, made numerous errors that could be attributed to an inadequate background. His estimate of the altitude of Pike's Peak missed the mark by 4,000 feet, and his reading of a nearby latitude erred by about thirty-five miles.[3] Moreover, Pike and the other explorers depended primarily on the will and curiosity of one man, President Jefferson for their support. The government gave them no institutional underpinning.

In the decade after Jefferson's presidency the government established the basis for the professionalization of official exploration. In 1816 topographical officers, known as geographers during the Revolution and as topographical engineers during the War of 1812 and thereafter, were added to the peacetime Army. Unlike the other officers of the Corps of Engineers, whose primarily military duties centered on the construction and maintenance of fortifications, "topogs" performed essentially civil tasks as surveyors, explorers, and cartographers. Two years later the War Department established the Topographical Bureau under Major Isaac Roberdeau to collect and store the maps and reports of topographical operations. Like the topogs, who numbered only six at this early date, the Bureau was placed under the Engineer Department.[4]

Almost from the outset there was a great demand for the skills of the topographical engineers. The accelerated movement of Americans into the interior of the continent served to emphasize the nation's need for networks of transportation and communication. Congress recognized the compelling nature of the requirement in 1824 by passage of the General Survey Act. This law, which authorized surveys for a national network of internal improvements, became the basis for heavy topog involvement in the development of canals, roads, and later railroads.[5]

Along with the growing importance of the topogs came increases in their numbers and improvements in the organizational structure. Most of the changes came during the first decade of Colonel John J. Abert's tenure as chief of the Topographical Bureau. A strong-willed and ambitious West Pointer who received the appointment after Roberdeau died in 1829, Abert sought independence for both the Bureau and the topogs. He realized the first goal in 1831, when Congress removed the Bureau from the Engineer Department and gave it departmental status under the Secretary of War. Seven years later he attained the second objective and became chief of an independent Corps of Topographical Engineers, a position he held for twenty-three years. Free of Engineer Department control and consisting of thirty-six officers, the organization of 1838 was a far cry from the handful of topogs in 1816.[6]

John J. Abert. *National Archives.*

Colonel Abert sought a great deal more for the topogs than prominence within the bureaucracy. While Roberdeau had been content to manage the office as a depot for maps and instruments and as a clearinghouse for correspondence, Abert saw his role as a planner and administrator for national policy regarding internal improvements and western exploration. As a member of the Board of Engineers for Internal Improvements, established to evaluate projects considered under the General Survey Act, Abert had a part in the selection of tasks and their execution.[7] In western exploration, which for many years took a back seat to internal improvements, Abert's role remained minor. His Bureau distributed instruments, collected maps, and forwarded correspondence.

Individual members of the Corps of Topographical Engineers, however, achieved great importance in western exploration and surveys. During the expansionist era of the 1840's, from the first stirrings of Oregon fever in the early years of the decade to the acquisition of the huge southwestern domain after the Mexican War, topogs examined the new country and reported their findings to a populace eager for information about the lands, native peoples, and resources of the West. Best known of all was John C. Frémont, the dark-eyed and flamboyant Pathfinder who led three parties to the Rockies and beyond during this age of expansion. The ranks also included William H. Emory, author of a perceptive assessment of the Southwest, and James H. Simpson, discoverer of the ruins of the ancient pueblo civilization of New Mexico. Howard Stansbury, whose report of an exploration of the Great Salt Lake is still considered a frontier classic, also wore the gold braid of the Corps of Topographical Engineers. In the 1850's, when the emphasis shifted from reconnaissance to more detailed exploration and roadbuilding, topogs continued to make their marks. John N. Macomb laid out the basic road network of New Mexico, and George H. Derby initiated harbor improvements in California, while Joseph C. Ives became the first Anglo-American to descend the Grand Canyon.

The disparity between the renown of members of Abert's Corps and the obscurity of his Bureau was due to the absence of a government policy regarding exploration. Topographical Engineers frequently went into the new country on an *ad hoc* basis, at the behest of a politically powerful figure like Missouri Senator Thomas Hart Benton, or to accompany a military expedition. From Major Stephen H. Long's 1819 journey up the Missouri River as a minor adjunct of Colonel Henry Atkinson's Yellowstone Expedition to Emory's southwestern exploration with the Army of the West during the Mexican War, Topog exploration often took a secondary position to other purposes.

When exploration and surveys in the trans-Mississippi West were finally organized and coordinated in the 1850's, Abert no longer wielded the political influence that had brought his ambitions so near fruition in the 1830's. Duties he hoped would devolve on the Topographical Bureau went instead to the Office of Pacific Railroad Explorations and Surveys, created by Abert's political foe, Secretary of War Jefferson Davis.[8]

Consequently, the story of topog explorations and surveys in the West was generally that of individual officers' achievements instead of a Bureau accomplishment. For Colonel Abert, their attainments represented a vision only partly fulfilled.

Despite the lack of a unified policy and central direction, the apparently episodic history of topog expeditions forms a coherent entity. Topographical officers provided the necessary link between the first explorations of the mountainmen—those rude, brawling beaver trappers who first probed far beyond the frontier and were no less than walking storehouses of geographical knowledge—and the civilian scientific specialists who undertook a rigorous study of western natural history and resources after the Civil War. Between the beavermen of the American Fur Company and the sophisticated specialists of the United States Geological Service, topogs provided the nation with an overall picture of the trans-Mississippi region. They explored bits and pieces as opportunity allowed until a coherent general understanding of western topography emerged in the form of Lieutenant Gouverneur K. Warren's map of 1857. His achievement, the first accurate overall depiction of the trans-Mississippi West, was a milestone in American cartography. Thereafter, topog activity centered on filling in the few blank spaces in Warren's map. During the Civil War, the Corps of Topographical Engineers was merged into the Corps of Engineers, whose officers renewed the topogs' efforts after Appomattox. Within a few years, however, civilian scientists took over the work and carried it forward. By then the officer-explorers had done their major task. They had extended and codified the knowledge of the mountainmen and in turn laid the groundwork for scholarly analysis. The Topographical Engineers had performed an essential service to a nation growing in size and in its understanding of itself.

Notes

1. William H. Goetzmann, *Exploration and Empire: The Explorer and the Scientist in the Winning of the American West* (New York: Alfred A. Knopf, 1967), p. 6.
2. *Ibid.*, pp. 44-45; Goetzmann, *Army Exploration in the American West 1803-1863* (New Haven: Yale University Press, 1959), pp. 35-39.
3. Marshall Smelser, *The Democratic Republic 1801-1815* (New York: Harper & Row, 1968), p. 130.
4. Edward Burr, "Historical Sketch of the Corps of Engineers, United States Army, 1775-1865," *Occasional Papers*, No. 71 (Fort Belvoir, Va.: Engineer School, 1939), pp. 33-39.
5. Forest G. Hill, *Roads, Rails & Waterways: The Army Engineers and Early Transportation* (Norman: University of Oklahoma Press, 1957), pp. 47-49.
6. Burr, "Historical Sketch of the Corps of Engineers," pp. 39-41; Herman R. Friis, "John J. Abert," *Dictionary of American Biography*, I, pp. 2-3.
7. Garry D. Ryan, "War Department Topographical Bureau, 1831-1863, An Administrative History," unpublished Ph.D. dissertation, American University, 1968, p. 79.
8. Goetzmann, *Army Exploration*, pp. 341-42, 346.

Chapter I

ACROSS THE FATHER OF WATERS

Steamboats were novelties on the western rivers in 1819, so any steamer docked at St. Louis that spring would have evoked interest. But the strange vessel that bobbed gently in the Mississippi River caused more than the usual commotion. One of the first sternwheelers on the river, the *Western Engineer* was remarkable for its shallow draft—a mere nineteen inches—and for its unusual adornments. A St. Louis newspaper described the vessel, the prow resembling "a huge serpent, black and scaly, . . . his mouth open, vomiting smoke," the trappings designed "to attract and awe the savage." The writer noted "artillery; the flag of the republic; portraits of a white man and an Indian shaking hands; a calumet of peace; a sword . . . ."[1]

The passengers were also out of the ordinary. The list was headed by Major Stephen H. Long, a Topographical Engineer and former West Point instructor. No stranger to St. Louis or the Mississippi, Long had ranged far up and down the river in 1817, selecting sites for Fort Smith on the Arkansas River and Fort St. Anthony at the confluence of the Minnesota and Mississippi. His companions included Dr. William Baldwin, physician and botanist; Augustus E. Jessup, geologist; Titian R. Peale, artist and naturalist; and zoologist Thomas Say.[2]

Major Long's party was the scientific branch of the Yellowstone Expedition, a large force sent by the War Department to secure the American claim to the upper Missouri River. British agents, "tools of a corrupt government," according to surgeon John Gale of the expedition and many of his countrymen, still worked among the Indians, cementing tribal loyalties to the Crown and channelling the peltry trade through Canada. President James Monroe and Secretary of War John C. Calhoun sought to eliminate British influence among the tribes of the northern plains. Although overshadowed by the main expedition, Long's scientific party had an important mission. Long's orders read: "explore the country between the Mississippi and the Rocky Mountains"—"permit nothing worthy of notice to escape your attention."[3]

On June 21, amid rumors that the crew would steam up the Missouri to its headwaters, dismantle the vessel, portage it over the Rockies, and sail down the Columbia, the *Western Engineer* left St. Louis and headed up the Missouri. The pace was leisurely. Speed averaged less than three miles

1

per hour, and now and then the boat tied up to put parties ashore. At Franklin, where the citizenry turned out to welcome "Long's Dragon," the group tarried a week, enjoying frontier hospitality and presenting their hosts with the town's exact latitude and longitude. Some pleasant times notwithstanding, the trip was no excursion. Heat, insects, and thieving Indians proved bothersome. Sickness plagued the expedition, and Dr. Baldwin, a consumptive, died. The river, with its snags, sandbars, and swift currents, was a navigator's nightmare. Yet, the *Western Engineer* got through. October found Long's company snug in winter quarters near Council Bluffs, at a place they called Engineer Cantonment, and Long himself en route to Washington to discuss plans for the following year.[4]

The winter at Engineer Cantonment was a significant chapter in the education of the scientific gentlemen. While examining the Council Bluffs vicinity, collecting natural history specimens, and taking astronomical observations for latitude and longitude, they learned of life on the upper Missouri. Here on the cutting edge of the frontier, where white and Indian cultures met, were the mountainmen, dirty and unkempt fur traders who were mostly illiterate and always wise to the ways of the wilderness. Joshua Pilcher, Lucien Fontenelle, and the most remarkable of all the early entrepreneurs in the trade, Manuel Lisa, visited the expedition's quarters. Lisa was extremely influential among the Indians and has been credited with personally sustaining the tenuous American foothold beyond the Father of Waters. These meetings marked the first intersection of the paths of Engineer-explorers and the mountainmen, two groups that would form a vital partnership in making available to all citizens an understanding of the great West. There were also the Indians, their faces streaked with red and white clay, who came to the camp to dance and share feasts of roast buffalo hump. Throbbing

Kansas Indians dancing for Major Long's party, 1819. *Library of Congress.*

2

drums, booming artillery, and the sizzle of broiling skunk all underscored the distance from the Philadelphia Academy of Natural Sciences.[5]

The Rocky Mountains from the Platte River. *Library of Congress.*

In the spring, Long's scientific party left the main expedition for a rapid reconnaissance across the plains to the Rocky Mountains. They moved westward along the Platte—a stream so sluggish that some men claimed its waters were not drinkable but edible—to the front ranges of the Rockies in what is now Colorado. Riding south along the eastern slopes of the mountains, they discovered and named Long's Peak, and pitched camp near the future city of Denver. After climbing Pike's Peak and measuring its height, the company split into two groups for the homeward journey, one going down the Arkansas, the other searching for the sources of the Red.[6]

Neither division successfully completed its mission. Long mistook the Canadian River for the Red and only discovered the error after going so far east that he could see the Ozarks. The trouble that beset the other party was vastly different. At the end of August, three soldiers deserted with the party's supplies, Indian presents, and scientific notes. Neither the manuscripts nor the miscreants were ever located.[7]

Nevertheless, the exploration had significant results, all beneficial save one. An account of the journey, compiled by Baldwin's replacement, Dr. Edwin James, disseminated much authentic information about vast areas of the West. A display of natural history specimens at Peale's Philadelphia Museum attracted crowds of curiosity seekers, and thus served to acquaint the public with rocks, plants, and animals from beyond the Mississippi. Major Long's map, which supplied fresh detail and corrected serious errors, became standard for a generation. Unhappily for his reputation, Long fixed the label Great Desert on the high plains and pronounced the region "almost wholly unfit for cultivation and, of course, uninhabitable by a people depending on agriculture for their subsistence."[8] Others before and after Long took much the same view, and with good reason. Early frontiersmen, dependent upon forests and streams, would have found the plains inhospitable, to say the least. Even so, Long went down in history as the author of the "Great American Desert" myth and as a delaying influence on western settlement.[9]

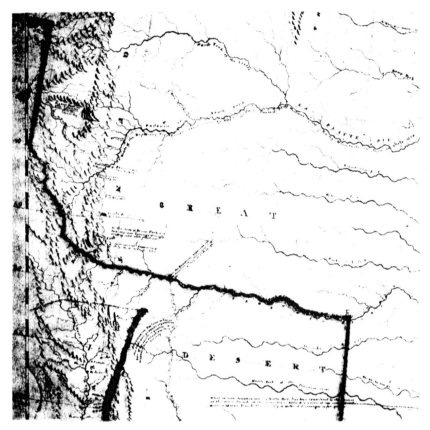

This portion of Long's map of his 1819–1820 expedition bears the label "Great Desert." *National Archives.*

During the two decades that followed Major Long's expedition, the government focused its efforts on the vast triangle west of the Mississippi, north of the Missouri, and south of Canada. Competition with Britain for both the peltry trade and loyalty of the Indians remained a potent motivation for several years. Then, as settlers entered Michigan, Wisconsin, and Minnesota, conflicts among the Indians themselves took on a new importance, for intertribal warfare endangered the nascent Anglo-American communities. Rumors of rich metal deposits on the shores of Lake Superior and an ongoing fascination with discovery of the source of the Father of Waters also stimulated interest in the Northwest. For these reasons, and because much of the trans-Mississippi Southwest

4

was controlled by a hostile Mexican government, the few expeditions that could be equipped and dispatched in the 1820's and 1830's probed the lands north and west of St. Louis.

Trained personnel for a thorough study of the Northwest were in short supply. The United States Military Academy educated nearly all civil engineers, and demand for their professional skills was heavy. Important projects closer to the centers of population, such as surveys of the Atlantic coast and Great Lakes and examination of routes for wagon roads, canals, and later railroads, required attention. The War Department, particularly under Secretaries John C. Calhoun in 1817-1825 and Lewis Cass in 1831-1836, was steadfastly committed to exploration. Nevertheless, the pressing need for an interior network of communication and transportation took precedence.[10]

Both internal improvements and western exploration were also limited by a lack of money. Although the primarily agricultural economy of the nation did not generate great wealth, the reluctance of Congress and the President to commit revenues to such programs was a far greater obstacle than an overall scarcity of funds. The widespread uncertainty in the government regarding the constitutionality of spending public money on internal improvements and exploration combined with sectional jealousies to block many proposals.[11] Consequently the expeditions of the 1820's and 1830's were frequently designed as multipurpose enterprises, so that they would be acceptable to congressmen reluctant to furnish money for exploration. Then funds to pay guides, buy Indian gifts, and obtain other essential goods and services had to be scraped from the bottom of the budgetary barrel. Because the expeditions were burdened with numerous responsibilities and could obtain only marginal financial support, the 1820's and 1830's were the lean years of Engineer exploration in the West.

The first expedition to follow Major Long's reconnaissance of 1819-1820 amply illustrated the conditions under which exploration would take place. In the autumn of 1819, while Long was struggling for funds to continue his work, Governor Lewis Cass of Michigan Territory suggested to Secretary of War Calhoun a probe of the south shore of Lake Superior and the waterways connecting the lake to the Mississippi. Mindful of the difficulties of obtaining support for exploration, Cass listed a number of other justifications for the expedition he intended to lead: an inquiry into Indian customs, acquisition of land for a military post at Sault Ste. Marie, examination of copper deposits along Lake Superior, and evaluation of Britain's role and influence in the fur trade. Cass requested a military escort, "an intelligent officer of engineers," and "some person acquainted with zoology, botany, and mineralogy." Aware that no funds were allocated explicitly for exploration, he asked Calhoun to authorize the expenditure of $1,000 to $1,500 from appropriations for Indian affairs.[12] Of such complicated expedients was born the exploring expedition of 1820.

Secretary of War Calhoun, always eager to obtain information about

5

the new country, approved Cass' proposal and provided the necessary personnel and assistance. He offered the post of mineralogist to Henry R. Schoolcraft, a versatile young naturalist "of more than ordinary vigor, daring, and perseverence," who had independently visited and studied the lead mines of Missouri in 1818. As topographer, Calhoun chose Engineer Captain David Bates Douglass, a graduate of Yale College who had served with distinction in the War of 1812. Douglass temporarily left his post as Professor of Natural History at the Military Academy to join Cass and Schoolcraft at Detroit in early May.[13]

On 20 May 1820, the thirty-seven scientists, soldiers, voyageurs, and Indians stepped into three canoes for the journey to the western tip of Lake Superior. Up Lake St. Clair, the St. Clair River, and Lake Huron to Michilimacinac and Sault Ste. Marie, they dipped their paddles rythmically in the cool, clear northern waters. After obtaining Ojibway approval for a military post at Sault Ste. Marie, Cass and his party followed the south shore of Lake Superior to "the far famed Copper Rock" of the Ontonogon, said by some early travelers to be a veritable mountain of pure copper. Both Douglass and Schoolcraft were disappointed by the quality and purity of the ore in the ten-cubic-foot lump, and made only a cursory probe for other deposits. They pushed their birch craft back into the water and paddled west into the wind, past the Bad, the Brule, and Iron rivers, to the mouth of the St. Louis at the western tip of Superior, where they beached their canoes forty-five days after leaving Detroit.[14]

Cass negotiated with the Indians, while Schoolcraft and Douglass devoted their time to scientific pursuits. Although unable to study deposits en route as carefully as he would have liked, Schoolcraft picked up enough samples to conclude that the south shore of Lake Superior would ultimately yield vast riches of copper, iron, and lead. Douglass carefully traced the route of the expedition but found time to "botanize and mineralize" as well. He also paid careful attention to the political relationships and loyalties involved in the fur trade. After coming close to discovering the source of the Father of Waters, the scientists returned to Detroit in September with promises of loyalty from numerous bands of Indians and a great wealth of geological, topographical, and ethnological information. Through Schoolcraft's account of the journey and numerous newspaper and magazine articles, the government and people of the United States learned a great deal about the new country, its native peoples, and resources—at a bargain price.[15]

Although Governor Cass was pleased, he was far from satisfied. After he returned to Detroit, he urged Secretary Calhoun to send other expeditions into the Northwest. Cass gave highest priority to reconnaissances of the St. Peter's (or Minay-Sotor, and later Minnesota), the most important tributary of the Mississippi above the Missouri, and the St. Croix rivers. Cass said both could be carried out by an able officer and ten men in a canoe. With this letter Cass in effect set the immediate goals for further exploration of the Northwest. The next two expeditions, sent by Calhoun in 1823 and by Cass himself as Secretary of War in 1832, did just what Cass suggested in 1820.[16]

Major Stephen Long commanded the 1823 expedition to the St. Peter's. Like Governor Cass three years earlier, Long led a low-budget, multipurpose enterprise. Instructions from the War Department required him to describe the topography of the country, fix the latitude and longitude of all important points, examine the regional fauna, flora, and minerals, and investigate the character and customs of the Indians. The source of funds was as complex as the mission. Less than one-tenth of the $2,000 allotted for the expedition actually came from the Engineer Department budget. Most of the money was taken from the Quartermaster and Indian departments, while the Subsistence Department contributed its share for such inedibles as steamboat and stage fare for landscapist Samuel Seymour and zoologist Thomas Say. Thus instructed and financed, Long set out again for the new country.[17]

The exploration began at Fort St. Anthony, near the mouth of the St. Peter's. There Long and his companions rested, enjoyed the hospitality of post commander Colonel Josiah Snelling, and added three interesting characters to the party. Frontier-wise fur trader Joseph Renville signed on as guide and interpreter, and Colonel Snelling's son Joseph volunteered to go along as Renville's assistant. Italian linguist and jurist Giacomo Costantino Beltrami, who had come up the Mississippi seeking its source, also joined the expedition. These three widely different people—a skilled frontiersman, an adventuresome officer's son, and a European scholar armed with a red umbrella—marched with the party when it left the post to follow the St. Peter's to the Red and Pembina.[18]

Long's sketch of the confluence of the Minnesota and Mississippi Rivers, from his 1823 journal. *Minnesota Historical Society.*

A month's journey, made alternately pleasant and miserable by handfuls of wild raspberries and swarms of mosquitoes, brought the expedition to the Scottish immigrant community of Pembina. Long spent five days at the small border settlement, observing the stars for latitude and marking the boundary with Canada. To the apparent satisfaction of the residents, all but one of the town's sixty log buildings stood south of Long's line. On 8 August 1823, Major Long formally took possession of the settlement for the United States, raised the stars and stripes, and fired a salute.[19]

On the next day Beltrami and Long quarreled and parted. Their disagreement flared when Long invited an Indian into their quarters. Beltrami turned the guest out. Long's protest of this unnecessary and foolish provocation only incited Beltrami to more foolishness. The Italian left in a huff, and headed southeast, accompanied only by two Ojibway guides and a Canadian-Indian interpreter. Beltrami came very near to finding the source of the Mississippi on his return trip. The lake he named Julia, for Countess Guilia Spade de Medici, was only a few miles from the true source. The state of Minnesota later commemorated his nearly successful quest by naming after him a county south of Lake of the Woods.[20]

While Beltrami went southeast, Long began his return trip by way of the northern lakes. After eighty-four portages his canoes glided into the blue velvet of Lake Superior. At Thunder Bay he crossed to the south shore so geologist William H. Keating could examine the Michigan copper deposits that had disappointed Schoolcraft and Douglass in 1820. Keating thought the deposits were so vast as to be inexhaustible. In time to come, his countrymen found reason to agree: in their first thirty-five years of operation, from 1855 to 1889, the Michigan mines produced over one trillion pounds of refined metal.[21]

Nine years after Long returned from Pembina, Henry Schoolcraft organized another multipurpose expedition into the north woods. Schoolcraft, then working as the Office of Indian Affairs agent to the northern tribes, sought an end to the frequent Ojibway-Sioux wars that threatened new settlements in the Northwest. He also wanted to investigate the influence of British traders on these conflicts. When he broached the plan to Secretary of War Cass, he asked that an Engineer officer accompany him to map the route of the expedition. Cass approved but was unable to provide an Engineer because of the great demands elsewhere for the skills of Corps officers. Instead Lieutenant James Allen, an infantry officer detailed to topographical duty, joined Schoolcraft to make the map, as well as report on geology and natural history, game and fish. Before Schoolcraft left, his tasks expanded to include a thorough study of the fur trade and even vaccination of the Indians against smallpox. Moreover, he had still another purpose in mind. After receiving his orders, he told Cass, "If I do not see the 'veritable source' of the Mississippi this time, it will not be from a want of effort."[22]

8

Schoolcraft and Allen, with Dr. George Houghton and about thirty voyageurs and infantrymen, followed the Cass-Schoolcraft route of 1820 to the head of Lake Superior. Twenty-three days later, after travel unlike anything experienced by Allen and his foot soldiers—around portages, through swamps, and over rapids—they stood on the shore of Lac la Biche, the true source of the Father of Waters. Schoolcraft renamed the lake Itasca, a word he coined from the Latin *veritas caput* ("true head"). On an island in the lake, dubbed Schoolcraft by Lieutenant Allen, the party hoisted a flag, which they left flying when they began their return. They made their way back to Superior via the St. Croix, which they followed from its mouth on the Mississippi to its source in northwestern Wisconsin. With their survey of the St. Croix they finished the basic reconnaissance suggested by Cass in 1820. On August 26 they arrived at Sault Ste. Marie, the exploration completed.[23]

Henry Schoolcraft at Schoolcraft Island in Lake Itasca. *Minnesota Historical Society.*

Although they passed rapidly through the north country, Schoolcraft and his companions accomplished a great deal. Equipped only with a compass, Allen accurately traced the party's route and drew the first map of the lake country in which the Father of Waters had its origin. Dr. Houghton vaccinated over 2,000 Ojibways and took a census of all the bands he met. So encouraging was Houghton's success that the government decided to continue efforts to protect the Indians against smallpox. Some bands promised to stop the constant intertribal warfare, but Schoolcraft harbored no illusions regarding a permanent peace. And, while he failed to stop the long-standing Indian feud, he scored a major triumph when he discovered and named "the 'veritable source' of the Mississippi."[24]

Secretary of War Cass could take great satisfaction from the exploration of the north country between 1820 and 1832. In spite of the lack of personnel and money, the general contours of the region had been made known, the copper deposits verified, and the source of the Mississippi identified. After his success in planning and executing the basic reconnaissance of the upper Mississippi and its major tributaries, the St. Peter's and the St. Croix, Congress for the first time became a willing collaborator in continuing exploration of western lands. In 1834 and again in 1836, while Cass was still Secretary of War, the national legislature voted $5,000 for geological and mineralogical surveys of western lands.[25]

With this money Cass authorized Colonel John J. Abert, chief of the Topographical Bureau, to hire George W. Featherstonhaugh to examine the mineral deposits in Arkansas Territory and then along the St. Peter's in Minnesota. Featherstonhaugh was an English traveler and geologist who had founded the short-lived *Monthly American Journal of Geology and Natural Science* in 1831. Secretary Cass, who well understood the utility of geological exploration, took an interest in the Englishman's work. Cass tried unsuccessfully to convince Congress to appoint Featherstonhaugh professor of geology at the Military Academy, before obtaining authorization to send him to the Arkansas frontier in 1834.[26]

Featherstonhaugh's two journeys across the Mississippi had few noteworthy results. In Arkansas he located some coal and lead deposits and cautioned pioneers against wasting effort in search of nonexistent deposits of precious metals. On his northwestern trip of 1835, his major achievement was identification of the coal deposits of western Maryland and Pennsylvania. After he arrived in Minnesota, he examined the St. Peter's with so much care that Joseph N. Nicollet, the brilliant French scientist who undertook an expedition sponsored by the Topographical Bureau in 1838, thought it unnecessary to add anything to the Englishman's analysis.[27]

Three years after Featherstonhaugh's return from Minnesota, Colonel Abert's bureau sponsored the first of two expeditions by Nicollet. Renowned in France as a mathematician, the former professor at the College Louis-le-Grand and one-time secretary of the Paris Observatory undertook on his own to explore and map the huge Mississippi basin. In the course of his travels, he improved on Schoolcraft's work by locating and tracing the courses of the small creeks that flowed into Lake Itasca and accurately fixing the longitude and latitude of the lake. Secretary of War Joel R. Poinsett, who shared the commitment to exploration shown by his predecessors Calhoun and Cass, became interested in Nicollet's enterprise and arranged for sponsorship of the project by Colonel Abert's office.[28]

On the first of his two expeditions as a civil agent of the Topographical Bureau, Nicollet examined the lush valley of the Minnesota and some of its tributaries. A young civilian topographer named John Charles Frémont (who also obtained his position through Poinsett), German

Joseph Nicollet at a trading post on the Crow Wing River. *Minnesota Historical Society.*

botanist Charles A. Geyer, and guide Joseph Renville accompanied him up the Minnesota and Cottonwood rivers to the Red Pipestone Quarry south of the Flandreau. Behind them came several French voyageurs driving horsecarts full of gear. Nicollet eagerly anticipated his visit to the quarry, which provided the Sioux with clay for their ceremonial pipes, but listened skeptically when the Indians told of thunder and lightning greeting visitors to the site. After a descent into the valley that was marked by a severe thunderstorm and violent winds, Nicollet spent five days at the quarry, making careful astronomical observations for his map and collecting geological specimens. From Red Pipestone he led his men back to Fort Snelling (formerly Fort St. Anthony) and south to St. Louis before winter ended navigation on the upper Mississippi.[29]

Inscription Rock at the Pipestone Quarry. The "C. F." below Nicollet's name stands for Charles Frémont. *Minnesota Historical Society.*

In 1839 Nicollet turned his attention to the Dakota prairie. He and Frémont, who was developing an almost worshipful admiration for the man he called the Pilgrim of Science, boarded the American Fur Company steamer *Antelope* at St. Louis for the trip up the Missouri to Fort Pierre. Geyer, former Prussian artillerist Louis Zindel, and mountainman Etienne Provost, also accompanied Nicollet on the paddle wheeler as it struggled upstream against the strong spring current of the Big Muddy. Always a careful observer, Nicollet noticed that the Missouri had changed dramatically since the days of Lewis and Clark. Many of the landmarks described by those pioneers of western exploration had been swept away by the furious river, which the *Antelope* battled for seventy days before reaching Pierre.[30]

After hiring two prairie-wise guides, William Dixon and Louison Frenière, Nicollet turned his back on the river and rode north across the prairie toward Devil's Lake. Mosquitoes were everywhere, and Frémont, now a second lieutenant in the Corps of Topographical Engineers, complained of many meals flavored by "mosquito sauce piquante." The exuberant and lusty Dixon rode point for the party, reconnoitering the land and picking the route. He led Nicollet through ravines and over hills toward a bluff overlooking the valley of the James River. Once atop the eminence, Nicollet understood Dixon's choice of paths. Before them lay the spectacular vista of the James, enlarged by the waters of the Mud, Snake, Nixon, and Wolf rivers, tributaries that joined it like spokes of a wheel while it wound through the Dakota prairie to the Missouri. Nicollet gazed in awe, while Dixon exclaimed, "Well, come now, you want geography: look! there's geography for you."[31]

Nicollet approached his fieldwork and computations with a meticulous professionalism. Stopping to sleep only three or four hours each night, he made over two hundred precise sets of astronomical observations for longitude and latitude and as many barometric readings for altitude. Armed with this data and other field notes on the topography, Nicollet travelled to Washington at the conclusion of the second expedition. There with the help of Frémont and another topog, Lieutenant Eliakim P. Scammon, the Frenchman worked long hours over many months translating rough sketches and field computations into his now famous map of the upper Mississippi valley.[32]

While Nicollet and his assistants toiled on the map, Colonel Abert pleaded with Congress for continued support of the project. He had sent Nicollet out in 1839 with only promises of an appropriation from Congress, then had to wait until 1840 to obtain money to pay the expedition's debts. Ultimately both Abert's faith and Nicollet's labors proved worthwhile. His chart of the hydrographic basis of the upper Mississippi fully met Abert's expectation of "an extremely accurate map."[33] Members of the American scientific community later echoed Abert's judgment. Spencer F. Baird, Assistant Secretary of the Smithsonian Institution, referred to his copy of the map as "highly prized," and Lieutenant Gouverneur K. Warren, an outstanding cartographer in his own right, called it "one of the greatest contributions ever made to American geography."[34] More recent commentators have only added to the encomiums of nineteenth-century critics.[35]

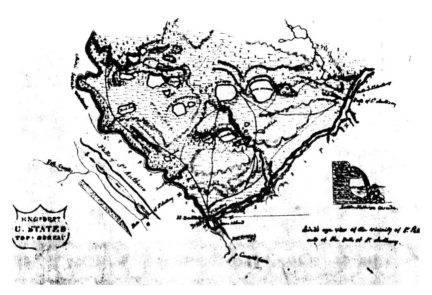

Nicollet's map of the confluence of the Minnesota and Mississippi Rivers. *National Archives.*

Publication of the map in 1843, shortly after Nicollet's death, capped a long and difficult period of exploration in the Northwest. The expeditions of the 1820's and 1830's accomplished complex missions with slender financial resources. Slowly, building on the Cass plan for exploration and then going beyond it, the Army obtained a complete picture of the huge region between the Missouri and Canada. While this process was underway, the underpinnings were laid for future efforts. The explorers made contacts with the knowledgable mountainmen and gained valuable experience in fieldwork; the Topographical Bureau gathered experience in administering the work. Like the Bureau, the Corps of Topographical Engineers was also growing to maturity. At least three topogs, Major Long and Lieutenants Frémont and Scammon, possessed a more than passing acquaintance with exploration, western cartography, or both. Thus, the decades of the 1820's and 1830's were both an end and a beginning. The reconnaissance of the Northwest was finished, and the topogs were ready for a larger role in exploration.

Notes

1. *Niles' Weekly Register*, 16 (July 24, 1819), 368.
2. Richard G. Wood, *Stephen Harriman Long, 1784-1864: Army Engineer, Explorer, Inventor* (Glendale, Calif.: Arthur H. Clark Company, 1966), pp. 27, 30, 37, 46, 52.
3. Goetzmann, *Army Exploration*, pp. 39-40; Wood, *Stephen Harriman Long*, pp. 61, 73; J. Franklin Jameson, ed., "The Correspondence of John C. Calhoun," *Annual Report of the American Historical Association*, 2 (1899), p. 159; E. W. Gilbert, *The Exploration of Western America, 1800-1850, An Historical Geography* (New York: Cooper Square, 1966), p. 159; Roger L. Nichols, ed., *The Missouri Expedition 1818-1820: The Journal of Surgeon John Gale with Related Documents* (Norman: University of Oklahoma Press, 1959), p. 3.
4. Wood, *Stephen Harriman Long*, pp. 79-84; Stanley Vestal, *The Missouri* (Lincoln: University of Nebraska Press, 1964), pp. 53-55; *Niles' Weekly Register*, 17 (October 8, 1819), 96; Goetzmann, *Army Exploration*, p. 41; John T. Starr, "Long's Expedition to the West," *The Military Engineer*, 53 (March-April 1961), 116.
5. Edwin James, *Account of an Expedition from Pittsburgh to the Rocky Mountains*, I (Ann Arbor: University Microfilms, 1966), pp. 153-63, 180-93; Goetzmann, *Exploration and Empire*, pp. 18, 57.
6. Wood, *Stephen Harriman Long*, pp. 77-91.
7. Wood, *Stephen Harriman Long*, pp. 105, 107, 109; James, *Expedition to the Rockies*, II, pp. 63, 167, 234-35.
8. Wood, *Stephen Harriman Long*, pp. 112, 118-19; Carl I. Wheat, *Mapping the Transmississippi West, 1540-1861* (San Francisco: Institute of Historical Cartography, 1958), p. 80; James, *Expedition to the Rockies*, II, p. 361.
9. For a discussion of the Great American Desert myth see Walter Prescott Webb, *The Great Plains* (New York: Grosset & Dunlap, 1957), pp. 147, 152-60.
10. Goetzmann, *Army Exploration*, pp. 13-14; Forest G. Hill, *Roads, Rails, & Waterways*, pp. 20-21, 143, 212, 214; Francis Paul Prucha, *Broadax and Bayonet: The Role of the United States Army in the Development of the North-West 1815-1860* (Lincoln: University of Nebraska Press, 1967), p. 189.

11. Carter Goodrich, "National Planning For Internal Improvements," *Political Science Quarterly*, 63 (March 1948), 36, 39; George Rogers Taylor, *The Transportation Revolution 1815-1860* (New York: Harper & Row, 1968), pp. 20-21.

12. Sydney W. Jackman and John F. Freeman, eds., *American Voyageur: The Journal of David Bates Douglass* (Marquette: Northern Michigan University Press, 1969), pp. 114-17.

13. George P. Merrill, *The First One Hundred Years of American Geology* (New York: Hafner, 1964), p. 68; Mentor L. Williams, ed., *Narrative Journal of Travels Through the Northwestern Regions of the United States Extending from Detroit through the Great Chain of American Lakes to the Sources of the Mississippi River in the Year 1820 by Henry R. Schoolcraft* (East Lansing: Michigan State College Press, 1953), p. 15; Charles B. Stuart, *Lives and Works of Civil and Military Engineers of America* (New York: D. Van Nostrand, 1871), pp. 199-200; Jackman and Freeman, eds., *American Voyageur*, p. 9.

14. Jackman and Freeman, eds., *American Voyageur*, pp. 58-59, 67; Henry R. Schoolcraft, *Narrative Journal of Travels from Detroit Northwest through the Great Chain of American Lakes to the Sources of the Mississippi River in the Year 1820* (Albany: E. & F. Hosford, 1821), pp. 175-76.

15. Jackman and Freeman, eds., *American Voyageur*, pp. xviii, 21, 79; Williams, ed., *Narrative of Schoolcraft*, p. 21, Schoolcraft, *Narrative Journal*, pp. 186-87; 199, 292-93.

16. Williams, ed., *Narrative of Schoolcraft*, pp., 321-22.

17. Secretary of War John C. Calhoun to Major S. H. Long, 25 April 1823, Letters to Officers of Engineers, Vol. 1, National Archives, Record Group 77; Major Long to Chief of Engineers, Major General Alexander Macomb, Letters Received, Engineer Department, National Archives, Record Group 77; Williams, ed., *Narrative of Schoolcraft*, p. 322.

18. Stephen H. Long, "Journal," Long Papers, Minnesota Historical Society; Evan Jones, *The Minnesota, Forgotten River* (New York: Holt, Rinehart, and Winston, 1962), p. 70; Wood, *Stephen Harriman Long*, p. 126; Augusto P. Miceli, *The Man with the Red Umbrella; Giacomo Costantino Beltrami in America* (Baton Rouge: Claitor's Publishing Division, 1974), pp. 35, 46.

19. Long, "Journal"; Theodore Christianson, "The Long and Beltrami Explorations in Minnesota One Hundred Years Ago," *Minnesota History Bulletin*, 5 (November 1923), 263; Miceli, *The Man with the Red Umbrella*, p. 80.

20. Joseph N. Nicollet, *Report Intended to Illustrate a Map of the Hydrographical Basin in the Upper Mississippi River*, 26th Cong., 2d sess., Senate Document 237, p. 59; Long, "Journal"; Wood, *Stephen Harriman Long*, p. 129; Miceli, *The Man with the Red Umbrella*, pp. 13, 71, 80-81, 83.

21. Wood, *Stephen Harriman Long*, pp. 130, 134, 136; Christianson, "The Long and Beltrami Explorations," 264; Merrill, *First One Hundred Years of American Geology*, pp. 104-05.
22. Philip P. Mason, ed., *Schoolcraft's Expedition to Lake Itasca: The Discovery of the Source of the Mississippi* (East Lansing: Michigan State University Press, 1958), pp. xii, xiv-xvi, xix, 139-40.
23. James Allen, *Report of Lieut. Allen and H.R. Schoolcraft's Visit to the Northwest Indians in 1832*, 23d Cong., 1st sess., House of Representatives Document 323, pp. 3, 7, 30, 32-33, 35-37, 44, 54, 57, 62; Mason, ed., *Schoolcraft's Expedition to Lake Itasca*, p. xx.
24. Mason, ed., *Schoolcraft's Expedition to Lake Itasca*, pp. xxi-xxiii; Allen, *Visit to the Northwest Indians*, p. 5.
25. *Laws of the United States Relating to the Improvement of Rivers and Harbors from August 11, 1790 to March 4, 1913*, 62d Cong., 3d sess., House of Representatives Document 149, Vol. I, pp. 67-68, 76.
26. Leonard D. White, *The Jacksonians, A Study in Administrative History 1829-1861* (New York: Macmillan Company, 1956), p. 499; Merrill, *First One Hundred Years of American Geology*, pp. 136-38.
27. George W. Featherstonhaugh, *Report of a Geological Reconnaissance Made in 1835, From the Seat of Government, By the Way of Green Bay and the Wisconsin Territory, to the Coteau de Prairie, an Elevated Ridge Dividing the Missouri from the St. Peter's River*, 24th Cong., 1st sess., Senate Document 33, p. 95; Nicollet, *Hydrographical Basin of the Upper Mississippi River*, p. 11-12, 71.
28. Allan Nevins, *Frémont, Pathmarker of the West* (New York: Frederick Ungar, 1961), pp. 29-31; Mason, ed., *Schoolcraft's Expedition to Lake Itasca*, p. xxv; Nicollet, *Hydrographical Basin of the Upper Mississippi River*, pp. 56-59.
29. Nicollet, *Hydrographical Basin of the Upper Mississippi River*, p. 15; Allan Nevins, ed., *Narratives of Exploration and Adventure by John Charles Frémont* (New York: Longmans, Green, 1956), pp. 39, 41-44, 46; Jones, *The Minnesota*, p. 98; June Drenning Holmquist and Jean A. Brookins, *Minnesota's Major Historic Sites, A Guide* (St. Paul: Minnesota Historical Society, 1972), p. 109.
30. Nevins, ed., *Narratives of Exploration and Adventure*, pp. 46-47; Nicollet, *Hydrographical Basin of the Upper Mississippi River*, p. 33; Donald Jackson and Mary Lee Spence, eds., *The Expeditions of John Charles Frémont*, I (Urbana: University of Illinois Press, 1970), p. 50.
31. Nicollet, *Hydrographical Basin of the Upper Mississippi River*, pp. 43, 45, 52; Nevins, ed., *Narratives of Exploration and Adventure*, pp. 58-60; Jackson and Spence, eds., *Expeditions of John Charles Frémont*, p. 52.
32. Martha Coleman Bray, "Joseph Nicolas Nicollet, Geographer," in John F. McDermott, ed., *French Men and French Ways in the Mississippi Valley* (Urbana: University of Illinois Press, 1969), pp. 32, 34, 38, 40; Nevins, ed., *Narratives of Exploration and Adventure*, pp. 70-71.

33. John J. Abert, *Annual Report of the Topographic Bureau, 1839*, 26th Cong., 1st sess., House of Representatives Executive Document 2, p. 637.

34. Spencer F. Baird to Colonel Abert, 15 February 1850, Baird Papers, Smithsonian Institution; Gouverneur K. Warren, *Memoir to Accompany the Map of the Territory of the United States from the Mississippi River to the Pacific Ocean*, 33d Cong., 2d sess., Senate Executive Document 78, Vol. XI, p. 42.

35. Donald Jackson, Commentary Accompanying Map Folio, Jackson and Spence,eds., *Expeditions of John Charles Frémont*, p. 7; Hiram M. Chittenden, *The American Fur Trade of the Far West* (Stanford, Calif.: Academic Reprints, 1954), II, p. 639; Goetzmann, *Army Exploration*, pp. 73-74.

Chapter II

FRÉMONT AND THE SCREAMING EAGLE

The America of 1842 stood poised to become a continental nation. Driven by complementary expansionist visions, the agrarianism of Thomas Jefferson and the commercial-maritime outlook of John Quincy Adams, the nation had already taken huge strides across the Mississippi.[1] As president in 1803, Jefferson obtained the immense but ill-defined Louisiana Territory from financially hard-pressed France. In the next year, he sent Meriwether Lewis and William Clark through the new country to the Pacific Ocean, calling the nation's attention to the vast domain and establishing a basis for later claims to ownership of Oregon. Thirteen years after the return of Lewis and Clark, Secretary of State Adams negotiated a treaty with Spain in which the boundaries of Jefferson's purchase were clarified and Spain gave up its claim to the Oregon country. Russian pretensions to Oregon went the way of Spain's after promulgation of the Monroe Doctrine, a creation of Secretary Adams that warned off potential European colonizers. Only Great Britain, which occupied Oregon jointly with the United States, remained a competitor when Adams left the State Department for the presidency in 1829.

Throughout the 1820's and 1830's, Americans made great inroads into the Mexican Southwest and Oregon. The beavermen ranged over the Oregon country and found an agricultural paradise into which farmers and missionaries began to trickle. In the southwest, American traders gained first a foothold and then pre-eminence in the Santa Fe trade. Meanwhile, Texas broke loose from Mexico and sought entry into the Union. As American influence spread, it began to seem that these far-off regions would inevitably fall to the Republic.

In the 1840's the process of expansion rapidly accelerated. When it became plain that Mexico, a weak young nation wracked by internal strife, could not hold its northern provinces for long, anxiety over British and French intervention mounted. At the same time, American appetites were whetted by Commander Charles N. Wilkes's glowing descriptions of the ports of San Francisco and Puget Sound after his naval exploring expedition of 1841. Jeffersonian agrarian expansionists already sang the praises of fertile Oregon, but after the Wilkes expedition Americans with a commercial-maritime orientation also took notice.[2] The nation was no longer willing to wait until the tenuous bonds connecting New Mexico to Mexico, and Oregon to Britain, broke of their own accord.

19

Senator Thomas Hart Benton of Missouri was among those least inclined to allow nature to take its course. Benton's St. Louis, transformed from a sleepy French outpost to a frontier metropolis at the hub of the Missouri River and Santa Fe trade routes, faced westward to Oregon and New Mexico. As feisty on the Senate floor as he had once been with a dueling pistol, Senator Benton shared his constituents' vision. Eloquently and willfully he turned many of his countrymen's heads in the same direction. While declaring that "man and woman were not more formed for union, by the hand of God, than Texas and the United States are formed for union by the hand of nature," he also called for "thirty or forty thousand American rifles" to negotiate an end to joint occupation of Oregon.[3]

As the long-standing Oregon dispute came to a boil, Benton planned a major expedition under Joseph Nicollet. Aware that each new settler in Oregon strengthened the claims of the United States, Benton wanted the French scientist to examine the emigrant route to the jointly occupied territory. Few risked the long and hazardous journey, and some of those who did perished along the way. To increase the number of emigrants and enhance their chances of success, good maps and descriptive guides were desperately needed. With these ends in mind, Benton secured funds from Congress for an examination of the Oregon Trail.

Because Nicollet's health was failing, Senator Benton offered leadership of the expedition to Lieutenant Frémont. Benton first met Frémont when he and Nicollet came to Washington to complete their report and map. As guests at the home of Ferdinand R. Hassler, chief of the coast survey, the urbane, polished Frenchman and his dashing assistant moved in the best circles and became society favorites.[4] Among the houses they frequented was that of Senator Benton, who took an avid interest in their work. Soon a romance blossomed between Frémont and the Senator's daughter Jessie. In the face of stern opposition from Jessie's parents, including banishment of the young topog to a survey of the Des Moines River, they married secretly. After a burst of senatorial temper came reconciliation. Benton had gained as a son-in-law an experienced explorer who would collaborate in his expansionist scheme.

In May 1842, Frémont bade his wife and his father-in-law farewell and set out on his first major expedition. Although his instructions from Colonel Abert required only a scientific survey of the vast region between the Missouri River and the Rocky Mountains, Frémont knew "the object of this expedition was not merely a survey; beyond that was its bearing on the holding of our territory on the Pacific; and the contingencies involved were large." Benton wanted him to "open the way for the emigration through the mountains," by marking the path and demonstrating the government's support of Oregon-bound settlers. Thus, Frémont's journey would blend scientific exploration with the politics of western expansion.[5]

Before he left Washington, Frémont hired a skilled topographer. Red-faced and red-haired Charles Preuss had burst into the Benton home just before Christmas, 1841, clutching a recommendation from Ferdinand Hassler as an excellent map-maker. Unemployed and desperate to find support for his family, Preuss could only stammer incoherently, but Hassler's note, which advised Frémont to examine some of Preuss's maps, spoke for him. Duly impressed with the German's work, Frémont provided his needy family with Christmas dinner and offered Preuss employment on the still incomplete map of the Mississippi basin, computing latitudes and longitudes from astronomical observations. Preuss knew nothing of such work so Frémont, characteristically impulsive and generous, worked nights to do it for him. In the spring of 1842, Frémont and Preuss went to St. Louis together, a long and fruitful relationship ahead of them.[6]

While Frémont chose hunters and teamsters and purchased his supplies, veteran trapper Kit Carson arrived in St. Louis from Santa Fe with a fur caravan. After many years beyond the Mississippi, Carson felt uncomfortable in the relatively civilized little city. Unsure of his destination but certain that he had to move on, Carson took passage on a

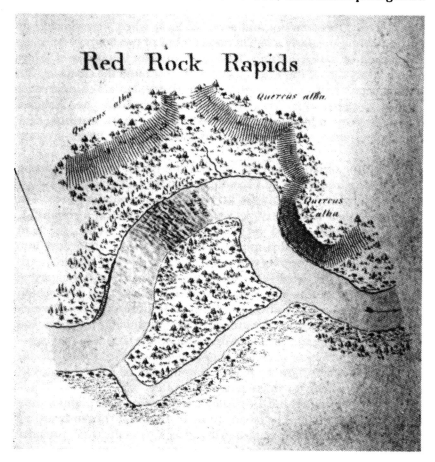

A portion of Frémont's map of the Des Moines River, done in 1841. *National Archives.*

21

steamer bound for the upper Missouri. On board he met Frémont, who still had not hired a guide. Carson later recalled: "I had been some time in the mountains and thought I could guide him to any point he would wish to go." Frémont signed him on, promising him the substantial monthly wage of $100.[7]

The meeting of the young officer and the experienced mountainman marked the beginning of an important friendship. Solidly built, with clear eyes and fair skin, Carson contrasted sharply with the smaller and darker topog. They were unlike in other ways too. While Frémont tended toward flamboyance and impetuosity, Carson was taciturn and methodical. Different though they were, Frémont and Carson became fast friends and important allies. Carson was to serve Frémont well on many explorations, while Frémont, by publicizing Carson's exploits as a trapper and guide, brought fame to the obscure mountainman.[8]

Accompanied by Carson, Preuss, and the rest of the party, Frémont left the riverboat at Choteau's Landing near present-day Kansas City for the march across the plains. The routine was rigorous: "At daybreak the camp was roused, the animals turned loose to graze, and breakfast generally over between six and seven o'clock, when we resumed our march, making regularly a halt at noon for one or two hours."[9] After the noon meal, the party continued westward until just before sunset. Then the muleteers turned the wagons into a circle around the campsite, the cooks collected fuel—wood when it was available, buffalo chips at other times—and started their fires, while others pitched tents and hobbled horses. Three-man guard details served two-hour shifts, watching over the camp as their comrades slept and the horses and mules browsed quietly.

The routine of daily marches and evening camps was interrupted a short distance from Choteau's Landing when the party faced the Kansas River, high, wide, and wild with the runoff from mountain snows. The men ferried their equipment across the swollen river on a collapsible India rubber boat carried for such a contingency. When the craft overturned, scattering provisions into the river, men on shore dove into the water, "without stopping to think if they could swim," and recovered most of the supplies. A few items, including much of the party's sugar and the precious coffee which warmed the men at their morning and evening campfires, were swept downstream. Frémont bemoaned the loss, "which none but a traveler in a strange and inhospitable country can appreciate."[10] The exhausted men dried out on the far side of the river—without their steaming cups of strong, sugar-sweetened coffee. On the next day all became right again, as Frémont chanced to meet a traveler who sold him twenty or thirty pounds of coffee.

The river crossing behind them, the party moved over the plains toward the valley of the Platte. The broad, uninterrupted vistas of gently rolling hills, with the tall buffalo grass bowing gracefully in the wind, provided security for the travelers. Yet in these grasslands, a neophyte's eyes could be deceived by distant objects, and twice the expedition's routine was

Kit Carson. *National Archives.*

broken by such sightings. Nine days west of the Kansas, a man in the rear peered over his shoulder, saw movement, and sounded the alarm "Indians! Indians!" Carson wheeled his horse to the rear and rode out to assess the danger. He returned shortly to tell his nervous comrades that the intruders were six elk. Preuss too fell victim to the plains, when near the Platte he halted to sketch a rare cluster of trees. To his astonishment the grove moved, and again it was Carson who identified the disturbing vision. Preuss had seen his first herd of buffalo. By the time the party reached the forks of the Platte, near the modern city of North Platte, all were wiser and more expert plains travelers.[11]

There the party split to meet again at the American Fur Company post of Fort Laramie. Frémont, Preuss, and four others followed the south fork into present-day Colorado to Long's Peak. After a brief meeting with a horse-hunting party led by black mountainman and one-time Crow chief James Beckwourth, Frémont and Preuss rode along the Front range of the Rockies to Laramie. Meanwhile, Carson led the main party directly up the North Platte.

While the party rested and bought supplies for the rest of the westward journey to South Pass and the Wind River range of the Rocky Mountains, Jim Bridger arrived at Fremont's camp. Already something of a mountain legend, "Old Gabe" knew as much about the northern Rockies as any man. He warned Frémont that hostile Sioux and Shoshone warriors would block the expedition's progress. Although urged by Carson and Laramie trader Joseph Bisonette to heed Bridger's words and turn back, Frémont decided to press on. Bisonette reluctantly agreed to accompany the party across the Laramie Plains to South Pass, but after six days on the trail his fears overcame him. Though all was still quiet, he turned back to Laramie, where his Indian wife and the homemade whisky known as Taos Lightning waited. The rest of the party, watched but not molested by the Indians, finished the journey to South Pass safely.

A week later, on 8 August 1842, Frémont found himself atop South Pass, the broad timberless path through the Rockies discovered in 1824 by mountainman Thomas Fitzpatrick. The gap surprised Frémont, for it had "nothing of the gorgelike character and winding ascents of the Allegheny passes in America; nothing of the Great St. Bernard and Simplon passes in Europe."[12] Instead, the grade resembled the ascent of Capitol Hill from Pennsylvania Avenue. Even Carson, despite his thorough familiarity with the country, had to search carefully to locate the pass.

Nearby began tributaries of the three great western river systems. From the eastern slope the North Platte and the Big Horn carried the melted snows into the Missouri, thence to the Mississippi and the Gulf of Mexico. On the west began the Green branch of the mighty Colorado, as well as the Snake, whose waters joined those of the Columbia on their way to the Pacific Ocean. And here, despite its undramatic appearance, was the most convenient route through the mountains, the gateway to Oregon.[13]

Descending the gentle western slope of South Pass, Frémont led his men into the Wind River range to mark the farthest point of his expedition with a dramatic flourish. On August 15, with a few companions and a specially made flag tucked inside his shirt, the topog struggled to the top of Snow Peak. With only moccasins on his feet, the thoroughly chilled but jubilant Frémont stood on the mountain's narrow snow-covered crest. There, in the stillness and solitude, he thrust a ramrod into a crevice and affixed his banner, with its star-encircled eagle clutching arrows and a peace-pipe, "to wave in the breeze where never flag waved before."[14]

A romanticized version of Frémont's ascent of Snow Peak, from Republican campaign literature of the 1850's. *Library of Congress.*

The same event, shown on a postage stamp issued in 1893. *Smithsonian Institution.*

The return trip should have been an anticlimax, but Frémont's recklessness nearly brought disaster on the Sweetwater River. A more prudent leader would never have put the India rubber boat into the turbulent stream, but Frémont was in a hurry. On August 25, the men climbed aboard and shot three small narrows, while Charles Preuss nervously clasped his chronometer and notebook to his chest. After a halt for breakfast, the boat sped over two falls without incident, but the water and foam that spilled over a third hid a large rock. Suddenly the boat overturned, throwing men and equipment into the white water. Preuss, still holding his timepiece and journal, struggled sputtering to shore. What he saw made him miserable: "Here floated a pack, there an instrument, there a sack; here an oar, there a coat, there a shirt." Almost everything was "gone to the devil." Then his eye caught the box which contained the expedition's precious books and records. Full of new hope, he waded neck-deep in the furious stream and retrieved it—empty. Angrily, he recorded his opinion of Frémont's management: "It was certainly stupid of the young chief to be so foolhardy where the terrain was absolutely unknown."[15]

By autumn the party was homeward bound. From a scientific standpoint, Frémont's results were seriously flawed: he had failed to fix the exact position of South Pass and, in his rash attempt to shoot the Sweetwater rapids, had lost some of his botanical and geological specimens. Politically, however, the impact of his journey could hardly have been sharper.

Frémont's report was a brilliant tour de force. Under pressure from

Congress for speed, he dictated the narrative to his talented wife, who added many elegant touches. By early 1843 all was ready. Published during the Senate debate on joint occupation of Oregon, the warm and enthusiastic report was snatched up by anxious readers and newspaper editors. Senator Benton's Missouri colleague, Senator Lewis F. Linn, also found immediate use for the report. From the floor of the Senate, Linn announced that the account "proves conclusively that the country for several hundred miles from the frontier of Missouri is exceedingly beautiful and fertile." This lush interior region, "alternate woodland and prairie," provided ample water for farming "in certain portions," and, most important, the valley of the Platte afforded "great facilities for emigrants to the west of the Rocky Mountains." Besides removing the label of Great American Desert from the central plains, the report gave would-be emigrants a trustworthy and detailed travel guide. After reading Frémont's account, an influential editor proclaimed: "All these foolish ideas . . . are to be dissipated—the bugbear is to disappear. . . . The nineteenth century will set upon a whole continent peopled by freemen."[16]

A second expedition, promptly agreed to by Congress, followed the successful journey to the Wind River range. In the spring of 1843, Frémont was busy organizing a party to go beyond the Rockies all the way to the Pacific. Once again he had both official and unofficial instructions. Colonel Abert directed him to follow a new route to South Pass and reconnoiter the region between the gap and the Pacific coast in Oregon. This would result in a complete survey of the interior and link Frémont's efforts with the 1841 naval reconnaissance of the coast by Commander Wilkes. Frémont's other directions came from Senator Benton, whose goals for the expedition were similar to those for the previous journey: the publicity generated would emphasize the importance of Oregon and stimulate interest in emigration and settlement.[17]

Frémont set out from St. Louis in the spring of 1843, carrying some scientific equipment—a telescope, sextants, chronometers, thermometers, barometers, and compasses—but also pulling a howitzer in his train. Frémont claimed that the small artillery piece, obtained through Colonel Stephen Watts Kearny from the arsenal at St. Louis, was intended for protection against Indians. However, other exploring parties successfully passed through the hunting grounds of powerful tribes without such armament. In fact, the howitzer might be valuable in the territory of another nation, and Frémont was bound not only for Oregon but for the Mexican province of California.

Colonel Abert in Washington was furious when he heard that Frémont had obtained an artillery piece. Abert ordered the lieutenant to Washington for an explanation, but Frémont never received the summons. He was camped near Choteau's Landing when Jessie received the order at the Benton home in St. Louis. She hastily scribbled a note to her husband, telling him to leave on his exploration immediately.

As soon as an exhausted rider brought Jessie's message, Frémont hitched up his twelve-pounder, broke camp, and set out for Bent's Fort on the Arkansas. Topographer Preuss, some forty armed muleteers, mountain men, and laborers, and scout Thomas Fitzpatrick, a ruddy-complected, white-haired veteran of the beaver streams who was called Broken Hand, marched with him. Frémont also had twelve two-mule carts full of gear and a light canvas-topped wagon with a good suspension to protect the instruments from the jolting cross-country trek.[18] Part way to Bent's trading establishment, Frémont sent Fitzpatrick and the wagons up the North Platte to Fort Laramie for supplies and arranged a rendezvous at Fort St. Vrain, a trading post north of modern Denver. Frémont cut south along the eastern fringe of Cheyenne country to the Arkansas and completed the journey to William and Charles Bent's outpost in mid-June.

Joined by Kit Carson at Bent's and resupplied by Fitzpatrick at St. Vrain, Frémont set out for the Great Salt Lake. On 6 September 1843, standing on a bluff above the Weber River, Frémont and Carson looked down on the lake Jim Bridger had discovered in 1824. The sight thrilled Frémont. Here was "the inland sea stretching in still and solitary grandeur far beyond the limit of our vision." Frémont followed Bear River down to the lake, and on September 7 his men penned the animals and prepared their rubber boat for a voyage on "the inland sea." That evening the explorers dined on yampa root and wild duck while a dazzling sunset that Frémont described as "golden orange and green . . . left the western sky clear and beautifully pure."[19]

The brief voyage on the lake and an equally cursory examination of the rivers that fed it from the northeast gave Frémont a favorable impression of the region, particularly of the valley of the Bear. Good grass, ample fresh water, timber, and salt all promised prosperity for cattle ranchers. The abundant bunch grass on the mountainsides, which nourished the beasts of the Indians and his own animals, could "sustain any amount of cattle and make this truly a bucolic region."[20]

Already beyond the region explored in 1842, Frémont hurried to complete his mission. Winter closed in on the north country as the party approached Fort Hall on the Snake. Determined to continue, Frémont assembled his men and offered them the opportunity to return home. Eleven left for the East, while the rest continued toward the Columbia, which they reached on October 25. They followed the river west to The Dalles, where Lewis and Clark had rested on their return from the Pacific, and established a base camp. Most of the men remained there, while Frémont and a polyglot group consisting of his black servant, Jacob Dodson, the German cartographer Preuss, a French-Creole voyageur, and three Indian guides paddled downstream in a canoe. Frémont was enraptured by the Columbia River valley, but Preuss hated it. On November 14 he recorded in his diary: "To hell with this country where it rains for five months." Frémont failed to notice his companion's bad humor. As the party floated foward Fort Vancouver, he jotted in his notebook: "A motley group, but all happy."[21]

After obtaining supplies from the generous Englishmen at Vancouver, Frémont returned to The Dalles and mustered his company for the southward journey to California. In mid-January 1844, the party faced the mighty snow-covered barrier of the Sierra Nevada range, standing tall and formidable between them and the green valley of the Sacramento River. Upon learning that Frémont planned to cross the mountains, the Indian guides gave up the enterprise as insane, leaving the party to face the knifelike wind and eye-stinging snow. For over three weeks they struggled upward, taking turns pounding the six-foot-deep snow with mallets so men and mules could continue the agonizing ascent. The mules became crazed with hunger and ate each other's tails and even saddle leather; the men in turn killed and ate the mules. February 23 was the nadir. The snow was so deep that it forced the party off the ridges onto the treacherous mountainsides, over which many of the men had to crawl to keep from falling. Frémont's feet gave way on an icy rock and he tumbled into a frigid stream. Carson leaped in after him, shared the bone-chilling bath, and pulled Frémont out.

On the following day, the exhausted and hungry band staggered over the summit. Ahead lay the green western slopes that led down to the valley of the Sacramento. Cheered by the sight, the party hurried to flee the snow-covered horror. The trial was over. After a brief and well-earned rest at Johann Sutter's New Helvetia ranch, Frémont was ready to continue his work.

During his short stay in California, Frémont accumulated a great deal of information for Senator Benton and his expansionist colleagues. In talks with Sutter and other American settlers, Frémont learned that the number of Americans trading with California ports and residing on ranches in the interior increased rapidly every year. The reasons for this growing migration were apparant. The soil was good, building materials abounded, and labor was cheap. No less clear was the hostility between the American ranchers and Mexican authorities on the coast. Many Americans talked of a revolt and independence from the weak and unstable government. It did not seem likely that Mexico could hold California for long.[22]

His inquiry completed and supplies replenished, Frémont set his course for home. He went south along the Pacific side of the Sierra Nevada, then through the montains via the San Joaquin River to the formidable Mohave Desert. The reconnaissance along the mountains disproved for Frémont the hoary myth of the Rio Buenaventura, a river thought to connect the Pacific at San Francisco to the interior. A myth was gone, but ahead lay the punishing reality of the desert. According to Frémont, the party suffered "intolerable thirst while journeying over the hot yellow sands ... where the heated air almost seems to be entirely deprived of moisture."[23]

They finally found a branch of the Virgin River, and then came across equally important aid in the person of mountainman Joseph Walker.

The veteran trapper guided the party the rest of the way around the southern edge of the Great Basin to the Sevier River and Utah Lake, just south of the Great Salt Lake. Frémont had circled—and named —the Great Basin after an eight-month journey of 3,500 miles.

While camped on Utah Lake, Frémont arrived at an understanding of the nature of the Great Basin. He perceived the region as a vast interior drainage system and returned home with the first comprehensive notion of its basic characteristics. The identification of the basin and the concomitant destruction of the myth of Buenaventura were among Frémont's greatest achievements as an explorer.[24]

His second report, as polished and informative as the first and even more exciting, had many avid readers. Large printings, public and private, gave the book wide circulation, and privately published guidebooks, such as Joseph E. Ware's *The Emigrant Guide to California*, drew heavily on Frémont's narrative. Abroad as well as at home, Frémont's report was warmly received. In London, the Royal Geographical Society heard Lord Chichester summarize the work. In Potsdam, the Prussian sage Alexander von Humboldt commended the author's "talent, courage, industry, and enterprise." At Nauvoo, Illinois, Brigham Young, swayed by Frémont's description, chose the area around the Great Salt Lake as the region his people would settle. And many a pioneer family, like that of Josiah and Sarah Royce, made its way to California "guided only by the light of Frémont's *Travels*." Writing to her absent husband in 1846, Jessie Frémont noted, "As for your Report, its popularity astonished even me, your most confirmed and oldest worshipper."[25]

An emigrant wagon headed for the Great Salt Lake. *Library of Congress.*

Frémont's sensational report included an excellent topographical map by Charles Preuss. The large sheet, which depicted the routes of both of Frémont's expeditions, was a cartographic milestone. By accurately representing the basic features of the new country, Preuss changed the course of western mapmaking. No longer would cartography be based on myth and speculation.[26]

In 1846 Preuss completed another map, more important for prospective emigrants than the first. On seven sheets he carefully traced the Oregon Trail, using Frémont's narrative to indicate campsites with essential grass, wood, and water and to show distances, climate, and Indian inhabitants. Widely popular among those who took the Platte River road to Oregon and California, this annotated atlas was one of the greatest contributions Frémont and Preuss made to the development of the West.[27]

Rewarded with a double brevet promotion to captain, Frémont planned his next expedition while war clouds gathered. Danger threatened from two quarters, Mexico and Great Britain. On 1 March 1845, shortly before he left office, President John Tyler signed a resolution annexing Texas, whose independence Mexico still refused to recognize. The new president, James K. Polk, elected on a platform claiming Oregon, also harbored designs on California. Vast empires were at stake and conflict seemed inevitable. Again the agent of expansionist politics, Frémont carried two sets of instructions as he assembled his party in St. Louis. His written orders were to survey the Arkansas and Red rivers, remain east of the Rockies, and return to the States before the end of the year. Actually, he was California-bound.[28]

A miniature Army—some sixty men in all, including artist Edward M. Kern, scout Joseph Walker, and many hardy veterans of past explorations—left St. Louis with Frémont. A dispatch to Carson brought him and his partner from their ranch near Taos. A band of Delaware Indians joined up, and so did some roving trappers. Soon the ranks swelled to nearly one hundred. Also with him were two inexperienced topogs, Lieutenant James W. Abert, the colonel's son, and Lieutenant William G. Peck. They and thirty men left the main party at Bent's Fort to reconnoiter the Kiowa and Commanche country. The rest went with Frémont: "A well-appointed compact party of sixty," he described them, "mostly experienced and self-reliant men, equal to any emergency likely to occur and willing to meet it."[29]

Late October found Frémont on the southern shore of the Great Salt Lake, in Mexican territory, ready to push across on the barren rugged expanse of the Great Basin. The view to the west was "nothing but mountains," serrated ridges running north and south. Looking out across their crests seemed to Frémont "like looking lengthwise along the teeth of a saw." Names he wrote upon the map—Pilot Peak, Humboldt River, and Walker Lake—marked his route through the desert, from watering place to watering place and from pass to pass. The region, with its stony, black mountains, sagebrush-covered floor, boiling springs, disappearing streams, and alkaline lakes deserved a thorough exploration, but, as Frémont afterward explained, "the time needed for it would interfere with other objects, and winter was at hand."[30] At the foot of the Sierra Nevada in late November, he divided his party, sending the main body under Kern

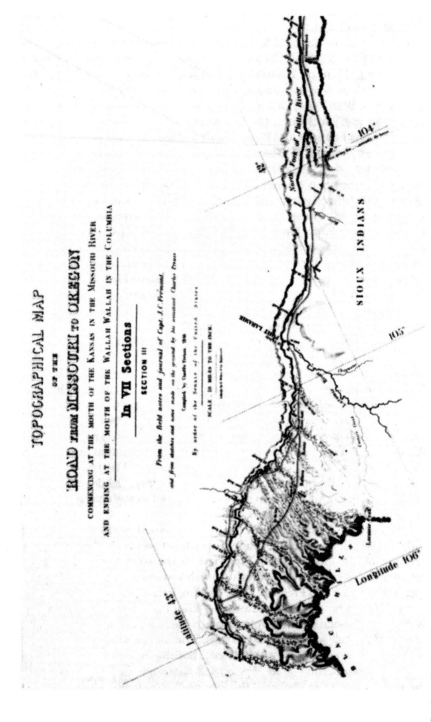

Section III of the Preuss atlas, showing the location of Fort Laramie. *National Archives.*

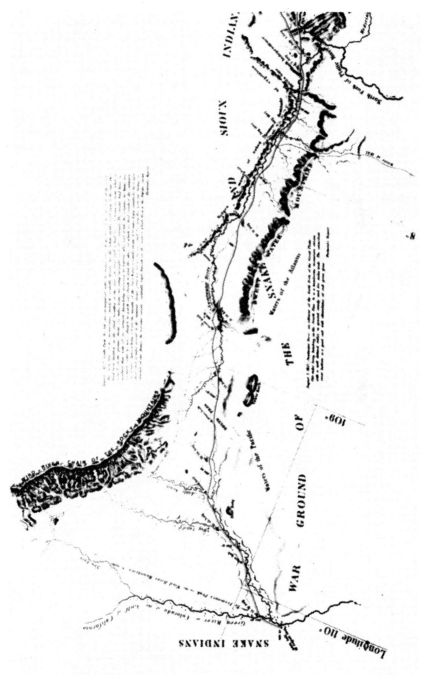

Section IV of the Preuss atlas, showing the location of South Pass. *National Archives.*

south to Walker's Pass and thence to the San Joaquin valley, while, with Carson and the Delawares, he struck over the mountains to Sutter's ranch. Reunited in California the following year, the party turned from exploration to conquest. With the United States at war with Mexico, the expedition formed the spearhead of the Bear Flag Revolt. As the nucleus of the California Battalion, a rag-tag, collection of frontiersmen and adventurers, Frémont and his men helped overthrow Mexican rule and hold the province until it could be occupied by the Army.

Frémont's career as a topographical engineer ended with his involvement in the conquest of Mexico.[31] While not deserving the title of pathfinder—that properly belonged to the frontiersmen who guided him through the river valleys and mountain passes—he marked the important trails on maps and in the minds of his countrymen.[32] His reports assaulted the notion of a Great American Desert, and dramatized the possibilities of Oregon, California, and the valley of the Great Salt Lake. An able agent of Senator Benton's expansionist politics, he provided accurate information on the vast new country for those bent on westering. When the American eagle was ready to make its screaming way to the shores of the Pacific, it followed the routes marked by Frémont.

Notes

1. William H. Goetzmann, *When the Eagle Screamed: The Romantic Horizon in American Diplomacy, 1800-1860* (New York: John Wiley & Sons, 1966), pp. 1-3.
2. Ray Allen Billington, *The Far Western Frontier 1830-1860* (New York: Harper & Row, 1962), pp. 145-48; Norman A. Graebner, *Empire on the Pacific: A Study in American Continental Expansion* (New York: The Ronald Press, 1955), pp. 219-20.
3. Frederick Merk, *Manifest Destiny and Mission in American History: A Reinterpretation* (New York: Alfred A. Knopf, 1963), pp. 37-38; Albert K. Weinberg, *Manifest Destiny, A Study of Nationalist Expansionism in American History* (Chicago: Quadrangle Books, 1963), p. 360; Thomas Hart Benton, *Thirty Year's View*, II (New York; Greenwood Press, 1968), p. 482.
4. Allan Nevins, *Frémont, Pathmarker of the West*, I, p. 56.
5. Nevins, ed., *Narratives of Exploration and Adventure*, pp. 81-82, 86; John C. Frémont, *Memoirs of My Life*, I (Chicago: Belford, Clarke, & Company, 1883), p. 69; Benton, *Thirty Years' View*, II, p. 478.
6. Frémont, *Memoirs of My Life*, I, p. 70; Nevins, *Frémont, Pathmarker of the West*, I, p. 93.
7. Milo Milton Quaife, ed., *Kit Carson's Autobiography* (Lincoln: University of Nebraska Press, n.d.), pp. 65-66; Morgan Estergreen, *Kit Carson, A Portrait in Courage* (Norman: University of Oklahoma Press, 1962), pp. 86-88.
8. Quaife, ed., *Kit Carson's Autobiography*, p. 66; Frémont, *Memoirs of My Life*, I, p. 74.
9. Nevins, ed., *Narratives of Exploration and Adventure*, p. 90.
10. Nevins, ed., *Narratives of Exploration and Adventure*, p. 91.
11. Erwin G. and Elizabeth K. Gudde, eds., *Exploring with Frémont, the Private Diaries of Charles Preuss, Cartographer for John C. Frémont on his First, Second and Fourth Expeditions to the Far West* (Norman: University of Oklahoma Press, 1958), p. 16.
12. Nevins, ed., *Narratives of Exploration and Adventure*, p. 126.
13. E.W. Gilbert, *The Exploration of Western America, 1800-1850, An Historical Geography* (New York: Copper Square Publishing, 1966), pp. 141, 143, 146, 149.
14. Nevins, ed., *Narratives of Exploration and Adventure*, p. 176.
15. Gudde and Gudde, eds., *The Diaries of Charles Preuss*, pp. 51-55.
16. Nevins, *Frémont, Pathmarker of the West*, p. 184; *Niles' Weekly Register*, 65 (October 28, 1843), 138.
17. Frémont, *Memoirs of My Life*, I. pp. 164-65; Nevins, *Frémont, Pathmarker of the West*, I, p. 127.

18. Leroy R. Hafen and W. J. Ghent, *Broken Hand, The Story of Thomas Fitzpatrick, Chief of the Mountain Men* (Denver: The Old West Publishing Company, 1931), pp. 138-40; Gudde and Gudde, eds., *The Diaries of Charles Preuss*, p. xxi.
19. Nevins, ed., *Narratives of Exploration and Adventure*, pp. 243-45.
20. Nevins, ed. *Narratives of Exploration and Adventure*, p. 258.
21. Gudde and Gudde, eds., *The Diaries of Charles Preuss*, p. 98; Nevins, ed., *Narratives of Exploration and Adventure*, p. 298.
22. Nevins, *Frémont, Pathmarker of the West*, I, pp. 164-71.
23. Nevins, ed., *Narratives of Exploration and Adventure*, p. 409.
24. Gloria Griffin Cline, *Exploring the Great Basin* (Norman: University of Oklahoma Press, 1963), pp. 214-16; Gilbert, *The Exploration of Western America*, pp. 171, 185.
25. John Caughey, ed., *The Emigrant Guide to California* by Joseph E. Ware (Princeton: Princeton University Press, 1932), pp. xi, xiii-xiv, xxiii; Goetzmann, *Army Exploration*, pp. 84, 108; Nevins, *Frémont, Pathmarker of the West*, I, p. 301.
26. Carl I. Wheat, "Mapping the American West," *Proceedings of the American Antiquarian Society*, 64 (April 1954), 103.
27. Goetzmann, *Army Exploration*, I, pp. 205-06.
28. Frémont, *Memoirs of My Life*, I, p. 423.
29. Nevins, ed., *Narratives of Exploration and Adventure*, p. 440.
30. Nevins, ed., *Narratives of Exploration and Adventure*, pp. 446, 453.
31. Frémont remained an important and controversial figure for many years. A quarrel with Colonel Stephen W. Kearny over command of American troops in California led to his court-martial and resignation from the Army. In 1848 he led a privately financed exploration for a railroad route to the Pacific and then entered politics, first as senator from the new state of California, and later as the first presidential candidate of the Republican Party. After commanding Union troops in Missouri during the early days of the Civil War and angering President Lincoln by prematurely liberating slaves, Frémont turned to railroad promotion. Numerous unsuccessful ventures were followed by six years as governor of Arizona Territory and finally, in 1890, by a place on the Army's retired list with the rank of major general.
32. Nevins, *Frémont, Pathmarker of the West*, I, p. 85.

Chapter III

THE MEXICAN WAR RECONNAISSANCE, 1845–1848

With the exception of the mountainmen, few Americans knew more about the Southwest in 1845 than they could find in a Santa Fe Trail guidebook. Up to that year, the Army had done little to explore and chart the region, which, except for the nine-year-old Republic of Texas, still belonged to Mexico. Commerical maps, frequently based on hearsay and conjecture, were woefully inaccurate. Even topog Lieutenant William H. Emory's 1844 map of Texas relied on the labors and—too often—the imaginations of earlier explorers and cartographers. The lack of reliable information became a major concern after Congress approved the annexation of Texas and war with Mexico became likely. Three expeditions, dispatched in the spring and summer of 1845 to examine the regions in which fighting appeared likely, passed through or skirted the Mexican provinces of New Mexico and California and inaugurated a long period of Engineer exploration in the Southwest.

The northernmost expedition stayed clear of foreign soil, but was nonetheless related to the dispute over the annexation of Texas. Because war with Mexico would make protection of the Oregon Trail difficult, a large force was sent to frighten the Sioux into allowing travelers to pass. Strung out in a column of twos behind Colonel Stephen Watts Kearny, 250 blue-clad horsemen of the First Dragoons made their serpentine way up the Platte to Fort Laramie, looking more like a punitive expedition than a reconnaissance. Only the presence of topog Lieutenant William B. Franklin, who accompanied Kearny to map the route, suggested anything but a warlike purpose.

Kearny's reconnaissance in force made a great impression on the Sioux. When told by a Fort Laramie trader that a large expedition would come up the Platte, they scoffed and called their informant a liar. Their disbelief turned to apprehension and fear of punishment for depredations when Kearny appeared at Laramie with his dragoons. Over one thousand Indians reluctantly responded to his demand for a conference. After watching the troops parade, flash their sabers, and fire their artillery, the Sioux readily agreed to allow the road to remain open and undisturbed.[1]

Up to the time of the meeting at Fort Laramie, Lieutenant Franklin, a bright young officer who graduated at the top of the West Point class of 1843, had little to do. Later he would map the route of the expedition's return by way of Fort St. Vrain and Bent's Fort, but the Oregon Trail needed no cartographer. Worn smooth by numerous emigrant parties and well publicized by Frémont, the route was fast becoming an early-day equivalent of an interstate highway. Franklin met and talked with numerous emigrants on their way to Oregon, most of them optimistic and in good spirits. As he conversed with them and promised to carry their letters back to the States, he learned that many of these pioneers had a clear vision of the nation's continental future. Though bound for Oregon, they had an eye on the land to the south, Mexican California. In Franklin's words,

> Very few of these people looked forward to staying in Oregon, but expected if they did not find very good land there, to push on to California, hoping as they said, that Uncle Sam would do something for them there one of these days.[2]

Oregon-bound settlers were not the only ones to share premonitions with Lieutenant Franklin. Old Soldier, a Northern Cheyenne chief who talked with the topog at the Indian village on Chugwater Creek, also saw clearly into the future. Although the systematic slaughter of the buffalo was yet to come and the whites did not present an immediate threat to his tribe's hunting grounds, Old Soldier foretold the tragedy that would overtake his people:

> He was very anxious to come to the States to see how the Eastern Indians live. He was convinced that something must be done by the Western Indians, as the buffalo were getting scarce, and unless they found some other way of living, they must starve. He was the only Indian whom I ever heard say anything on the subject, and we were sorry he could not come with us, perhaps it would have done a great deal of good.[3]

Like a few of the exuberant white pioneers, some among the doomed plains Indians also understood what was happening in the trans-Mississippi West.

Guided by Thomas Fitzpatrick on the more circuitous homeward route, the expedition made its way south along the eastern edge of Mexico's vast possessions. During the journey from Fort Laramie to Bent's Fort, the Arkansas River capital for the fur trading empire of Charles and William Bent, Franklin paid careful attention to the topography. He made daily notes on the direction and distance traveled as well as nightly observations for latitude.[4] Once a show of force, Kearny's expedition was now a reconnaissance.

For all except Fitzpatrick, the summer's work was nearly over once Kearny's troops turned eastward at Bent's Fort onto the Santa Fe Trail. Six days after the command struck the Santa Fe road, an express rider overtook Kearny with a letter from Frémont, who had just arrived at Bent's. Preparing to lead one exploring party into California and to dispatch another into New Mexico, Frémont wanted Fitzpatrick to serve as guide for New Mexico-bound Lieutenants Abert and Peck. Colonel Kearny, with his command on the clearly marked road to Fort

Leavenworth, released Fitzpatrick. Lieutenant Franklin, who watched with regret as the mountainman—"a perfect master of woodcraft," according to the admiring topog—departed, knew Fitzpatrick would be "a great acquisition to any party that may go into any part of the Far West."[5]

After a brief reunion at Bent's Fort, the discoverer and the chief publicist of South Pass went their separate ways. Frémont departed for the Great Basin and Humboldt River on an expedition that would place him in northern California when war broke out the following year. Fitzpatrick joined young Abert, the intelligent and sensitive son of the chief of the Topographical Bureau, for the journey into northeastern New Mexico. Although Abert was a tenderfoot explorer, totally unfamiliar with the country, he was a perceptive observer and a skilled artist. Moreover, with Fitzpatrick at his side, he knew his own ignorance of the terrain would be immaterial.[6]

Equipped with only a sextant and a chronometer, the Abert party set out to survey the Canadian River from its source high in the Sangre de Cristo range to its junction with the Arkansas near modern Tulsa. They followed the Purgatory River to its head near Raton Pass, gateway to Santa Fe for trading expeditions or an invading army, where the cool, clear water was a welcome change from the saline pools of the plains. As the men urged their mules along the streambed, luxuriant vines, ferns, and trees blocked the sun, reminding Abert of a tunnel "formed by the goddess Flora." "Almost wild with excitement," the party reluctantly left the Purgatory and sought the head of the Canadian.[7]

On the Purgatory, Lieutenant Peck learned something of the reliability of mules. The mainstays of many exploring parties, these ordinarily patient and durable beasts carried baggage, scientific instruments, and frequently explorers over the most difficult terrain in the foulest weather. As a last service, they sometimes provided famished men with a bad-tasting but desperately needed dinner. Unsung despite their important role in western exploration, they did not go uncursed, for they sometimes went their own way or refused to go at all. Lieutenant Peck joined the ranks of mule-hating ingrates after he dismounted to pluck a snack from a plum tree. Smacking his lips he started toward the tree. The mule, with Peck's gear and journals, set out in the opposite direction. The topog could only watch helplessly as the animal trotted away. Fortunately, other members of the expedition caught the truant, but Peck almost paid for this fruit with his mount, saddle, and notebooks.[8]

Although assigned primarily to a route reconnaissance, Abert examined the country carefully as he picked his way along the mountain trails. South of Raton Pass he located a good site for a military post, "should our government succeed in extending its territory to the Rio [Grande] del Norte" and he found ample evidence of gold-bearing rock.[9] Fearful of arrest as a trespasser by Mexican authorities, he never tarried to collect geological specimens. Instead he and his party followed the Canadian eastward out of the mountains to the Texas panhandle. Free of any danger from the Mexicans, Abert now faced an even greater menace, the Comanches.

Considered by many the finest horsemen in the world, these fierce and courageous people were rightly known as the lords of the southern plains. Masterful tacticians who would wait patiently out of range for a volley of musket fire before charging their reloading enemy, they waged war for plunder, status, territory, and the joy of a good fight. Even the Apaches, themselves bold and fearsome warriors, cringed before the superb Comanche cavalry. Lieutenant Abert, a newcomer to the hunting grounds of these tipi-dwelling nomads, knew before he left Bent's Fort that the Comanches "were greatly to be feared."[10]

The Comanches watched the party as it crossed the panhandle, and Abert, who saw their signal fires, knew it. The men remained constantly on the alert and were once nearly attacked by a band of Kiowas who mistook the explorers for the hated Texans who had come into their country and fought for the right to stay there. On another occasion, Abert convinced a few Comanches, who had followed at a distance, to visit his camp and share a meal. Baffled by the explorers, who had come neither to trade nor wage war, the Indians allowed them to pass unharmed.

Before leaving Comanche country, Abert almost made a potentially fatal mistake. He found a good sample of an Indian cranium and was about to add it to his specimens, when some frontier-wise members of the expedition convinced him to discard it. He would not have found it easy to explain possession of the skull to a Comanche chief.

The brief reconnaissance, which ended in October at Fort Gibson, Indian Territory, was useful in several ways. Abert produced an accurate map, which included the location of the three crucial means of survival in the wilderness—water, wood, and grass. He also supplied important information on the Comanches and Kiowas. Under the tutelage of Fitzpatrick, whom Abert credited with preservation of his party, he and Peck gained valuable field experience, which they would put to good use on their more extensive exploration of New Mexico in 1846.[11]

As he started east from Fort Gibson, Abert observed the same phenomenon that had impressed Franklin on the Oregon Trail. Everywhere he saw pioneer wagons bound for newly-annexed Texas. A trace of awe crept into Abert's journal as he noted the size of the migration into the new country:

> The way from Fort Gibson was literally lined with the wagons of emigrants to Texas, and from this time until we arrived at St. Louis we continued daily to see hundreds of them.[12]

In Bernard DeVoto's words, 1846 was "the year of decision." In that year several crucial events in the development of the trans-Mississippi West took place. The United States and Britain ended their joint occupation of the Oregon country and agreed to a division of the region. The first Mormon emigrants crossed the Mississippi on the long, tortuous road to their new haven in the Great Basin. And, in April, shots were fired along the Rio Grande, and the war with Mexico began.

As soon as hostilities opened, the administration of President James K. Polk moved to seize the Mexican provinces of California and New Mexico. The government directed Commodore John D. Sloat, commanding naval forces off the California coast, to take San Francisco and Monterey. At the same time, Colonel Kearny received orders to organize an invasion of New Mexico. Kearny and the 1,500 members of his Army of the West set out down the Santa Fe Trail from Fort Leavenworth in late June, 1846.

Included in the Army of the West was a topographical detachment commanded by Lieutenant William H. Emory, a red-whiskered, soldierly former artilleryman who became a topog in 1838. Like Frémont, he had good connections. His wife was Matilda Wilkins Bache, a great granddaughter of Benjamin Franklin and a sister of Alexander D. Bache, who succeeded Ferdinand Hassler as superintendent of the Coast Survey. Emory's circle of friends included Henry Clay, Jr., Jefferson Davis, and Maryland Senator James A. Pearce. A zealous explorer, fascinated with the history and ethnology of the Southwest, Emory was a good choice for the Kearny expedition.[13]

Although Kearny's large force had a purely military mission, the conquest of New Mexico and California, Emory availed himself of every opportunity to explore the countryside on the long march from Bent's Fort to Santa Fe and thence to San Diego. His staff was small, only three officers (young Abert, Peck, and Lieutenant William H. Warner), and two civilians (statistician Norman Bestor and artist John Mix Stanley). His hastily collected gear was scanty. Moreover, military duties had always to come first for, as Emory acknowledged, "war was the object," not investigation.[14] Yet through almost superhuman effort, he managed to carry out his inquiries. Aided by a dwindling number of assistants (Abert took sick on the trail and was left at Bent's Fort; Peck remained in Santa Fe to wait for Abert), he denied himself sleep to observe the heavens and fix geographic positions. Stops to collect specimens, survey "long-sought ruins," visit pueblos and Indian farms, and study the culture and customs of the native tribes interrupted each day's hard ride. "I am worked almost to death," he complained at one point.[15] But if the strain was great, so was the accomplishment.

From his careful scrutiny of the unfamiliar terrain, Emory arrived at several important conclusions. Although at places like the confluence of the San Pedro and Gila rivers "not an object in the whole view, animal, vegetable, or mineral had anything in common with the products of any state in the Union, with the single exception of the cottonwood...," Emory came to know the country well. He realized that New Mexico's limited agricultural potential would depend on irrigation, which in turn would require centralized community control—much like the procedures that the Mormons would shortly employ in the Great Basin. The scarcity

William B. Franklin. *U.S. Military Academy Archives.*

of fertile lands also meant that slavery would be unprofitable in the Southwest. The presence of a free, dark-skinned native population only underscored the problems slaveholders might face. With the Indian villages offering tempting refuge, control of bondsmen would be difficult indeed. Most important was Emory's discovery that the central government in Mexico City, unable to provide protection against the raids of Apaches and Navahoes, was little respected by New Mexicans of all classes. This was important intelligence. The conquest of the province, worthwhile because of the Santa Fe trade and the easy possibility of running a wagon road or railway across it to California, would meet little local resistance.[16]

William H. Emory. *U.S. Military Academy Archives.*

In addition to these shrewd observations, Emory produced the first accurate map of the Southwest. Later popular among gold-seekers who took the southern route to California, his map was based on hundreds of barometric readings and 2,000 nighttime astronomical observations. On the march during the day, Emory measured streams, calculated grades,

Santa Fe after occupation by Kearny's Army of the West. *National Archives.*

examined topographical contours, and recorded information on the climate. Unusual problems complicated his task. When he set up his horizon to measure altitudes, he found that the galloping of horses as far away as five hundred yards agitated the mercury in the instrument. This caused trouble throughout the journey, but particularly near villages of inquisitive Indians. Near the Pima village on the Gila, Emory wryly commented that "news got about of my dealings with the stars, and my camp was crowded the whole time." His accomplishments in the face of the many difficulties measured his persistence and dedication. Added to Joseph Nicollet's cartographic achievement in the north country, and the work of Frémont and Preuss in the Great Basin, on the Oregon Trail, and the Columbia River, Emory's map was the last building block for a basic understanding of the geography of the trans-Mississippi West.[17]

As the Army of the West marched along the Gila toward California, Emory and his topographical detachment, together with a small dragoon escort, led the way. At the confluence where the Gila's "sea green waters are lost in the chrome colored hue of the Colorado," the topogs met a party of herdsmen with about five hundred horses.[18] Their leader claimed to be employed by wealthy Sonora horsemen, but Emory was unconvinced and detained the entire group. On the next day, his suspicions were confirmed. He and Stanley stopped a well-mounted Mexican, on his way, he said, to hunt horses. Emory took the rider to Colonel Kearny, who ordered the Mexican searched. He turned out to be a courier from California with a packet of letters that identified Emory's earlier captive as a colonel in the Mexican Army, then enroute to General José Castro's army with his large herd of horses.

Emory's capture of the Mexican herd was the Army of the West's only contact with the enemy until the column neared San Diego. Confident of an easy passage to his destination, Kearny had divided his force. With many of his soldiers garrisoning Santa Fe and others invading Mexico under Colonel Alexander W. Doniphan, the once-formidable army was

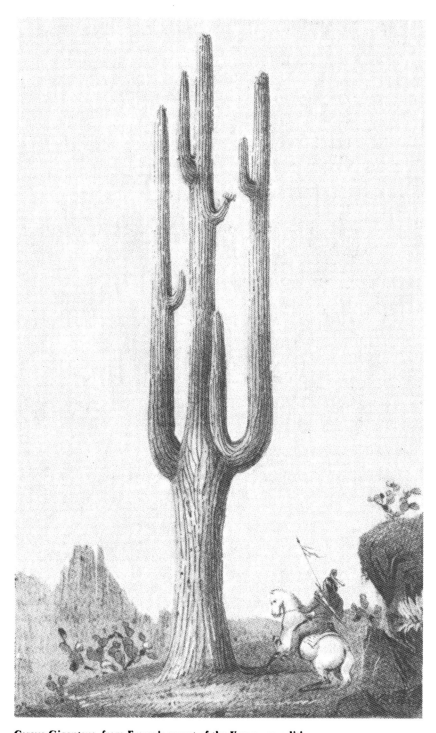

Cereus Giganteus, from Emory's report of the Kearny expedition.

reduced to a mere company of 160 hungry, bone-weary men. Challenged near modern Escondido by a fresh, well-mounted force of *Californio* cavalry, Kearny unwisely decided to stop and fight. Instead of drawing his troops into a compact formation and remaining on the road to San Diego, he led his men in a charge against the pike-wielding foe, gave them just the kind of fight they wanted, and paid dearly for it. The bitter hand-to-hand clash, known as the battle of San Pasqual, took eighteen American lives and left Kearny with a saber wound of the buttocks. After a marine detachment from San Diego reinforced his badly mauled army, Kearny made it to the coast. Technically victorious because he held the field after the Mexicans withdrew with their two dead, Kearny was lucky to escape with only his embarrassing scratch.[19]

The Army of the West on the march across New Mexico.

At San Diego, whose harbor Emory considered among the finest on the Pacific coast, many of the members of the expedition had their first view of the ocean. The vista was stunning. Few of the men had seen anything with which to compare the broad green expanse of water. One mountainman, groping for a metaphor, turned on its head the familiar comparison of the great plains with the ocean, exclaiming, "Lord! There is a great prairie without a tree."[20]

Emory had just left Santa Fe for the trek to California when Lieutenant Abert recovered from his illness at Bent's Fort. Alternately delirious with fever and despondent because of his condition, Abert whiled away the time on the Arkansas reading Horace, sketching Indians, and arranging his growing collection of natural history specimens. Employees of the Bents, who daily brought him rare plants and minerals, birds and fish, helped lighten the burden of enforced inactivity. Vexed nonetheless by his inability to resume active duty, Abert recorded his despair at "having come this far, and having been stopped just as I was entering upon a field full of interest to the soldier, the archeologist, the historian, and the naturalist."[21]

One of the drawings made by Lieutenant Abert during his convalescence at Bent's Fork in 1846.

The young topog spent much of his time at Bent's with the Southern Cheyennes who traded there. Renewing acquaintances with some whom he had met in 1845 and entertaining them by drawing their likenesses in his sketchbook, Abert learned a great deal about tribal life. Like their northern cousins, whom Lieutenant Franklin had visited on the Chugwater, the Arkansas River bands depended on the bison for their daily necessities. The meat was their basic food, the bones became their utensils, and the skins protected them from the savage plains winter. Also like their northern relatives, the wiser among them saw clearly the grim future. In conversation with the influential and farsighted Yellow Wolf, Abert learned of the decreasing numbers of buffalo on the southern plains and the corresponding decline of the tribe. "He says," Abert wrote after a conversation with Yellow Wolf, "that in a few years [the buffalo] will become extinct; and unless the Indians wish to pass away also, they will have to adopt the habits of the white people, using such measures to produce subsistence as will render them independent of the precarious reliance afforded by the game."[22] Sympathetic with their plight, Abert urged government assistance for the Cheyennes. The whites, with their continuous travel through the buffalo ranges, their evergrowing number of roads, and their hunts for buffalo robes, bore responsibility for the impending disaster. Neither the ailing topog nor the perceptive chief knew that, before any assistance came, the Cheyennes would have to endure Chivington and Custer, Sand Creek and the Washita.* Abert and Yellow Wolf were voices crying in the wilderness.

In early September, 1846, shod in antelope mocassins and astride a buffalo-skin saddle, Abert finally left Bent's for his rendezvous with Peck in Santa Fe. Again up the Purgatory and over Raton Pass. Abert guided his mule into New Mexico. Although he was retracing the route he had taken in 1845, the trip was not without some excitement. There were grizzly bears in the mountain passes, and rattlesnakes once spooked his mount. And there were huge masses of stratified rocks that were better historians than mortals could ever be. Fired with romantic enthusiasm, Abert examined these massive records of the past and pondered their significance:

> I could not but compare the legends these rocks unfold with the doubtful records of history. See with what detail they present everything to us, showing us specimens of birds, of plants, of animals, and the like, telling us when and where they existed. See how they go back ages upon ages! behold with astonishment the mighty deeds in which they have been concerned, the grand convulsions they have undergone.[23]

After Abert rejoined Peck, who had already examined the country north

---

*Major defeats inflicted on the Cheyennes by Colorado Volunteers in 1864 and by U. S. troops in 1868. See, for example, William H. Leckie, *The Military Conquest of the Southern Plains* (Norman: University of Oklahoma Press, 1963), pp. 22-24, 99-105.

of Santa Fe, they rode out to survey the settled Rio Grande valley. Guided by Emory's detailed instructions, they made a meticulous inquiry into the uses and possibilities of the region. In the saddle for nearly three months, Abert and Peck went from town to town, studying agricultural production, estimating population, and examining mineral resources. Whether on the road being pelted by large hailstones or sampling the peaches and melons of the Indian pueblos, they constantly scrutinized and recorded their surroundings. They finished their survey just before Christmas and returned to Santa Fe with detailed notes on the economy and resources of the Rio Grande valley, from Socorro to Santa Fe.

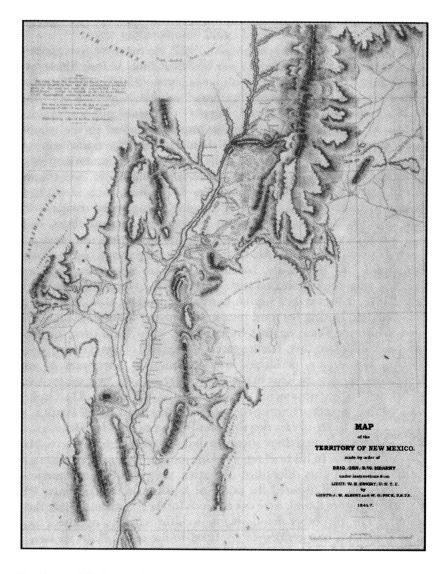

The Abert and Peck map of the Rio Grande valley. *National Archives.*

Abert's return to Fort Leavenworth proved far more difficult than either his illness or his survey. Struggling over the top of Raton Pass in a vicious snowstorm, with the wolves patiently following his almost exhausted men and animals, Abert faced the kind of winter that occasionally turned civilized men into cannibals. East of Raton, the weather grew worse. Stung by fierce north winds, their faces covered with frost, the men struggled eastward, while the mules moved in clouds of vapor as sweat evaporated from their hides. With one man snowblind and two dead—one had shot himself and the other had suffocated when snowdrifts collapsed his tent—Abert stumbled into Leavenworth on the first of March. As he boarded a Missouri River steamer for the next leg of the journey home, he looked back on his southwestern journeys "like the realization of some romance" and wondered "that I could have borne so much."[24]

As Abert wrote those lines in March, 1847, the romantic first phase of the southwestern reconnaissance was rapidly fading. Already Emory and Frémont had been under fire in different parts of California. Like their fellow officers in the Corps of Engineers (including Lieutenants George G. McClellan, George G. Meade, Pierre G. T. Beauregard, and Captain Robert E. Lee), many other topogs became involved in the combat operations of the Mexican War. While some surveyed the coastal waters of Texas and located supply depots for the invasion, others accompanied the attacking columns across the Rio Grande, surveying routes, constructing fortifications, and probing enemy lines. Still others, such as Captains Joseph E. Johnston and George W. Hughes, commanded troops in the campaign for Mexico City. In addition to these numerous duties, there was still surveying and mapping to be done—in the heart of Mexico.

Two surveys south of the Rio Grande, led by Hughes and by Lieutenant Edmund L. F. Hardcastle, became significant beyond expectations. Hughes, who entered Mexico with General John Wool's column in the fall of 1846, collected data similar to that obtained by Abert and Peck in New Mexico. During his tour, he also formulated the defense plan later used to protect Texas against Indian raids. Two years later, after the conquest of Mexico City, Hardcastle examined and mapped the Valley of Mexico. His survey, performed with instruments once used by von Humboldt, became an issue in the controversy over the annexation of all of Mexico, when opponents of expansion south of the Rio Grande claimed that he was preparing the way for a huge land grab.[25] Ironically, Hardcastle's matter-of-fact description of the campaign for Mexico City with its attendant map drew attention that should have been reserved for Captain Hughes. In his brief report of his journey through Coahuila and Chihuahua, Hughes identified lucrative possibilities for American entrepreneurs and assessed the political loyalties of the residents. The majority, Hughes found, were not anxious for the Americans to take their country. On the other hand, many wealthy citizens opposed their government. As one gentleman confided to the topog, "Sir, we have a glorious country and a good population but our government is the worst in the world. I would rather be under the dominion of a Comanche chief."[26] If either of the surveys of Mexican territory was an incitement to further expansion, it was Hughes's, not Hardcastle's.

In all, two-thirds of the thirty-six officers of the Corps of Topographical Engineers served in the field during the war. Colonel Abert spoke proudly of his officers, who, he said, showed "the versatility of talent in the Corps and its ability to fulfil any military duties which it may be found necessary or proper to assign to it."[27] Colonel Abert was right. As explorers and cartographers, naturalists and soldiers, the topogs were as much a part of the Mexican offensive as the officers and men of the line.

Notes

1. William B. Franklin, Report to Col. S. W. Kearny 1st Dragoons Commanding the Expedition to the South Pass of the Rocky Mts, November 5, 1845, Letters Received, Topographical Bureau, National Archives, Record Group 77; George E. Hyde, *Spotted Tail's Folk, A History of the Brulé Sioux* (Norman: University of Oklahoma Press, 1961), p. 34.
2. Franklin, Report to Col. S. W. Kearny.
3. Franklin, Report to Col. S. W. Kearny.
4. Franklin, Report to Col. S. W. Kearny.
5. Franklin, Report to Col. S. W. Kearny.
6. James W. Abert, *Report of an Expedition on the Upper Arkansas and through the Country of the Comanche Indians in the Fall of the Year 1845*, 29th Cong., 1st sess., Senate Document 438, p. 8. Unless otherwise indicated, the following account of Abert's expedition is based on this report. Footnotes are provided only for portions quoted in the text.
7. James Abert, *Expedition on the Upper Arkansas*, p. 16.
8. Nancy Alpert Mower and Don Russell, eds., *The Plains, Being No Less than a Collection of Veracious Memoranda Taken During the Expedition of Exploration in the Year 1845, From the Western Settlements of Missouri to the Mexican Border, and From Bent's Fort on the Arkansas to Fort Gibson, via South Fork of the Canadian, North Mexico and Northwestern Texas* by François de Montaignes (Norman: University of Oklahoma Press, 1972), pp. 82–83.
9. James Abert, *Expedition on the Upper Arkansas*, p. 19.
10. Ernest Wallace and E. Adamson Hoebel, *The Comanches, Lords of the South Plains* (Norman: University of Oklahoma Press, 1952), pp. 34, 47, 245, 258, 264, 290-92, 296; Rupert N. Richardson, *The Comanche Barrier to South Plains Settlement* (Glendale, Calif.: Arthur H. Clark, 1933), pp. 15, 26, 44; James Abert, *Expedition on the Upper Arkansas*, p. 2.
11. Warren, *Memoir*, p. 52; Goetzmann, *Army Exploration*, pp. 126-27.
12. James Abert, *Expedition on the Upper Arkansas*, pp.74-75.
13. Goetzmann, *Army Exploration*, pp. 128-30; Charles F. Cary, "William Hemsley Emory," *Dictionary of American Biography*, III, pt. 1 (New York: Charles Scribner's Sons, 1958), pp. 153–54.
14. William H. Emory, *Notes of a Military Reconnaissance from Fort Leavenworth, in Missouri, to San Diego, in California*, 30th Cong., 1st sess., Senate Executive Document 7, p. 50. Unless otherwise indicated, the following account of Emory's expedition is based on this report. Footnotes are provided only for portions quoted in the text.

15. Emory to Colonel John J. Abert, 16 December 1846, Letters Received, Topographical Bureau.
16. Ross Calvin, ed., *Lieutenant Emory Reports: A Reprint of Lieutenant W. H. Emory's Notes of a Military Reconnaissance* (Albuquerque: University of New Mexico, 1951), pp. 9-10; Emory, *Notes of a Military Reconnaissance*, p. 77.
17. Goetzmann, *Army Exploration*, p. 142; Kenneth R. Stunkel, "Military Scientists in the American West," *Army*, 13 (May 1963), 56; John J. Abert, *Report of the Chief, Topographical Engineers, 1847*, 30th Cong., 1st sess., Senate Executive Document 1, p. 657; Emory, *Notes of a Military Reconnaissance*, p. 87.
18. Emory, *Notes of a Military Reconnaissance*, p. 95.
19. Stephen Watts Kearny to the Adjutant General, 12 December 1846, and John M. Stanley to [?], 19 January 1847, in George Winston Smith and Charles Judah, eds., *Chronicles of the Gringos: The U.S. Army and the Mexican War, 1846-1848, Accounts of Eyewitnesses and Combatants* (Albuquerque: University of New Mexico Press, 1968), pp. 156-57, 159; Goetzmann, *Army Exploration*, pp. 139-41; Edwin L. Sabin, *Kit Carson Days 1809-1868*, II (New York: The Press of the Pioneers, 1935), pp. 526, 530-31.
20. Emory, *Notes of a Military Reconnaissance*, p. 113.
21. James W. Abert, *Report of Lieut. J. W. Abert of his Examination of New Mexico in the Years 1846-'47*, 30th Cong., 1st sess., Senate Executive Document 23, p. 3. Unless otherwise indicated, the following account of Abert's expedition is based on this report. Footnotes are provided only for portions quoted in the text.
22. James Abert, *Examination of New Mexico*, p. 6.
23. James Abert, *Examination of New Mexico*, p. 22.
24. Quoted in John Galvin, ed., *Western America in 1846-1847: The Original Travel Diary of Lieutenant J. W. Abert who Mapped New Mexico for the United States Army* (San Francisco: John Howell, 1966), p. 96.
25. Goetzmann, *Army Exploration*, p. 152; Edmund L. F. Hardcastle, *In Further Compliance with the Resolution of the Senate of August 3, 1848, Calling for a Map of the Valley of Mexico, by Lieutenants Smith and Hardcastle*, 30th Cong., 2nd sess., Senate Executive Document 19, pp. 2-14.
26. George W. Hughes, Descriptive Memoir of the Country from Monclova to Cinegos, 15 November 1846, Letters Received, Topographical Bureau.
27. John J. Abert, *Report of the Chief, Topographical Engineers, 1848*, 30th Cong., 2nd sess., House of Representatives Executive Document 1, pp. 324-25.

Chapter IV

BOUNDARY SURVEYS
SOUTH and NORTH

After the Mexican War the boundaries of the United States changed dramatically. By the Treaty of Guadalupe-Hidalgo, formally proclaimed by President Polk on Independence Day, 1848, Mexico gave up its claim to Texas and the vast domain that included what would become Utah, Nevada, and California, as well as much of New Mexico and Arizona. Larger than the Louisiana Purchase and almost the size of India, the cession, including Texas, added nearly 1,200,000 square miles to the United States. As diverse as it was large, the new country included the snow-capped sawteeth of the Sierra Nevada and the bone-dry floor of the Mohave Desert, the fantastic canyonlands of the Colorado and the verdant Rio Grande valley of New Mexico.

The Topographical Engineers' first major postwar assignment was surveying the border between the new domain and Mexico. A precise line had to be drawn over 1,800 miles of extremely rugged terrain. Shifting rivers, hostile Indians, and diplomatic disputes added to the difficult conditions. Requiring over six years to complete, the Mexican boundary survey would be one of the topogs' sorest trials.

Under the terms of the treaty, a joint American-Mexican commission would "run and mark the said boundary in its due course" from a point just south of San Diego to the mouth of the Rio Grande and agree to its exact location. Article Five of the compact defined the border as running up the Rio Grande all the way to El Paso del Norte. From this town, also called Paso and later Ciudad Juarez (it should not be confused with the neighboring Texan city of El Paso on the other side of the river), the line would extend westward to the Gila River, follow it to its junction with the Colorado, then run along the border between Upper and Lower California.[1]

Representing the United States was a mixed group, part civilian and part military, under control of Secretary of State James Buchanan. For the office of commissioner, President Polk chose lawyer John B. Weller, a former congressman from Ohio and recent unsuccessful candidate for governor of the state. In a second political appointment, Polk gave the surveyor's post to Andrew B. Gray, a Texan with limited experience in topographical work. For scientific talent, the commission drew on the Topographical Corps. Emory, now a brevet major, became the ranking military member with the title of chief astronomer, assisted by Lieutenant Amiel W. Whipple, who had spent five years on the northeastern boundary survey, and Lieutenant Edmund L. F. Hardcastle, who had mapped the Valley of Mexico in late 1847. The makeup of the commission gave little joy to northern Whigs and Free Soilers, who opposed the expansion of slave territory. Weller was a proslavery Democrat; Gray was friendly with promoters of a southern Pacific railroad; Emory, scion of a Maryland slave-holding family, advocated a Gila valley route for a transcontinental railroad; and Hardcastle, also a Marylander, was linked to the movement for annexing all of Mexico. With sectional rivalries becoming sharper and a Whig administration about to take office, the commission seemed headed for trouble.

Even before the American commission left New York, there were intimations of diplomatic troubles ahead. Both sides had accepted John Disturnell's 1847 map of North America as the basic reference document for the survey. A compiler but not a cartographer, Disturnell was well-known for his many guidebooks.[2] When his map proved faulty, the commission faced one of its most aggravating problems.

Engineer Lieutenant William H. C. Whiting discovered a major flaw in Disturnell's map while on a reconnaissance of western Texas. In March, 1849, while the commission sailed toward the Isthmus of Panama, Whiting fixed the true location of El Paso del Norte about thirty miles south of its position on the map. Since the Rio Grande line would end and the New Mexico boundary would begin at a point just north of the town, its location was of crucial importance.[3]

Ignorant of Whiting's findings, the members of the commission were having trouble enough. Arriving at Chagres in mid-March, they found the isthmus jammed with fortune seekers bound for the California El Dorado. Not until May could they complete their journey; and not until July, when the Mexican commission under General Pedro Garcia Conde arrived, could parties take the field. Meanwhile, soaring prices strained their funds, and visions of gold nuggets induced escorting troops to desert. Personal relationships also caused problems. While Weller established a cordial working relationship with his Mexican counterpart, he was less successful with his astronomer. Major Emory, unhappy with his subordination to political appointees and already gently cautioned by Colonel Abert to "avoid getting upon stilts,"[4] contained himself only with difficulty. When Weller and Gray met with the Mexicans at San Diego to plan operations eastward to the Gila, they refused to include Emory in the meeting because the treaty recognized only the commissioner and surveyor as official representatives. Emory contented himself with a short note of protest, and the initial point of the boundary was established in October.[5]

While Gray and Emory marked the initial point just south of San Diego with a stone monument, topogs Hardcastle and Whipple took parties east into the California desert. Hardcastle reconnoitered the country between the Pacific and the confluence of the Colorado and the Gila. Whipple, meanwhile, set out across California to erect a boundary marker at the junction of these rivers.

San Diego mission.

Because a survey by triangulation over the rugged Gila valley presented great difficulties, Emory's instructions required Whipple to fix his positions astronomically. After arriving on the river, Whipple built an observatory on an eminence he dubbed Capitol Hill, and commenced the series of astronomical observations necessary to establish the longitude and latitude of the boundary marker. He approached the painstaking and exhausting work with almost maniacal dedication. Observation of the stars at night and computations during the day left him drained and sometimes too nervous to sleep. On 25 November 1849, Whipple erected a stone pier that marked the point of the boundary at the mouth of the river.[6]

Whipple's report of his activities on the Gila concluded with a vocabulary of the Yuma Indian language.[7] Keenly interested in the southwestern tribes, he established an excellent rapport with them. The commander of his escort, dragoon Lieutenant Cave J. Couts, viewed such scholarly interest in the Yumas with astonishment and disgust. Snubbed and considered a nuisance by the aloof, bookish Whipple, the loquacious outgoing Couts dismissed the topog as "not worth a tinker's dam for anything under God's heaven" without his books.[8] Few officers, including Couts, matched Whipple's sensitive and sensible concern for the native population.

Too preoccupied to smooth Couts's ruffled feathers, Whipple was ever mindful of his principal tasks. Shortly after his arrival on the Gila, in a letter dated "Capitol Hill—Right Bank of Rio Colorado, opposite the mouth of Rio Gila," he alerted Emory to an important problem. In the course of a mere eight days, the wild-running Gila had already erased a long sandy point at its mouth. The river, designated by the Treaty as part of the boundary, did not always run in the same bed.[9] Therefore, as Emory said, "the survey of that river . . . fixes nothing, determines nothing . . . ."[10]

57

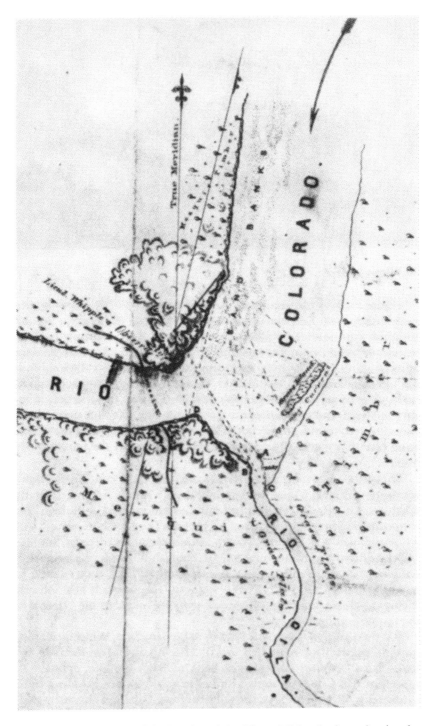

Lieutenant Whipple's map of the junction of the Gila and Colorado rivers, showing the lines of triangulation. *National Archives.*

Camp Yuma at the mouth of the Gila River.

While work progressed at San Diego and on the Gila, partisan politics caught up with the commission. First came rumors that the new Whig administration of President Zachary Taylor had replaced Weller with John C. Frémont. Local banks reacted by refusing to honor Weller's government drafts, and Emory, whose testimony at Frémont's celebrated court-martial had helped convict the pathfinder, threatened to resign. The situation stabilized when Frémont declined the post to become senator from California, and Weller stayed on until he ran out of funds in February, 1850.

The commission resumed its work in November with John Russell Bartlett, Rhode Island antiquarian and loyal Whig, holding forth as chairman. Bartlett's chief assistants were surveyor Gray and topog Lieutenant Colonel John McClellan, a hard-drinking veteran of the Seminole and Mexican wars.[11] Bartlett arrived on the frontier in style. He crossed the plains from Indianola, Texas, in a deluxe carriage with an escort of twenty-four armed horsemen. A nattily uniformed host of 170 soldiers, sailors, and civilians, among whom were scientists, cronies, and boondogglers, completed the huge contingent.[12] The commission, Emory later wrote,

> was oppressed with a multitude of officers, quartermasters, commissaries, paymasters, agents, secretaries, sub-secretaries—all officers wholly unknown to any well-regulated surveying corps, and worse than useless by the conflict of authority which these officers engendered, and the

59

enourmous expense which payment of their salaries and personal expenses entailed. . . .[13]

The first problem to test Bartlett's mettle was the location of the boundary at El Paso del Norte. The difficulty was exacerbated when Colonel McClellan's fondness for John Barleycorn led to his replacement by contentious Lieutenant Colonel James D. Graham. He was present when Bartlett and the Mexican commissioner discovered that Paso was considerably south of its presumed location. The two commissioners agreed to run the boundary north of the town's location on Disturnell's inaccurate map. Surveyor Gray, whose signature was required on any agreement, joined Graham and Whipple in a vigorous dissent. Their claim that south of the border would be too far north did not move Bartlett, who ordered the line run according to Disturnell's map.[14]

Shortly after this quarrel, the work got underway again. Bartlett sent Whipple to perform the pointless survey of the shifting Gila. Graham and topog Lieutenant William F. Smith began work on the Rio Grande portion of the boundary. Graham's party had trouble even getting started. In three raids, the Apaches and Navahoes ran off much of his livestock. Finally, Graham had to lead a raiding party of his own and managed to retake many of his horses and beef cattle.[15]

The Indian fights were only the first of Graham's difficulties. He complained loudly about the large number of placemen and boondogglers in Bartlett's retinue, the lack of sufficient instruments, and the difficulty of locating Bartlett, who had an uncommon talent for putting great distances between himself and the border he was supposed to survey. All of these problems annoyed Graham, but two in particular infuriated him. The first stemmed from the rescue of a Mexican girl, Inez Garcia, from Indians who had captured her in a raid. Instead of sending her home with a small escort, Bartlett took the entire party on the gallant but frivolous errand. His chivalry cost the commission forty-eight days. Already incensed, Graham grew still angrier when Bartlett insisted that Graham's position was confined to command the military contingent.[16]

The dispute was finally settled by the removal of both men. In September the disputatious Graham was relieved by Emory. Bartlett came under fire in the Senate for agreeing with Conde's demand for running the border far to the north of El Paso del Norte. Sparking the attack was former Commissioner Weller, the recently seated senator from California. In a fiery speech on 6 July 1852, Weller called for an investigation of his successor's conduct. Other lawmakers joined him in denouncing the Bartlett-Conde bargain. Emotions ran high. Lamenting the loss of the southern railroad route, a Texas senator declaimed: "There can be no sort of excuse for . . . giving away five or six thousand square miles . . . which properly belongs to us, which is ours by right, and which we should not surrender."[17] A provision impounding the commission's funds sailed through both houses. Recurrent cries of "Whig giveaway" helped produce a Democratic landslide in November 1852, as well as the dismissal of Bartlett and Gray.[18]

Meanwhile, Emory reached El Paso del Norte in November, 1851, and found the survey foundering. Faced with a lack of funds and Bartlett's burdensome party, he considered the situation "anything but agreeable."[19] To Professor Joseph Henry of the Smithsonian he confided his astonishment at the commissioner's large retinue and scanty financial resources: "Can he afford to keep all the people who are about him and pay the workies too!"[20] Emory soon knew the answer. Unable to meet the payroll, he faced a mutiny in his camp at Paso. Luckily, authorization to draw money reached Emory just after his party refused to proceed any farther. Then a merchant en route to San Antonio accepted Emory's draft for $5,000. Thus financed, Emory could pay his men, discharge the most troublesome among them, and continue the fieldwork.[21]

Under Emory's firm management, the survey of the Rio Grande began to progress rapidly and efficiently. Although the river made a clear boundary, a detailed examination was nonetheless needed for both defense and customs purposes. This was a difficult undertaking,[22] for, according to Emory, the Rio Grande was largely impassable,

> walled in at places by stupendous rocky barriers, and escaping through chasms blocked up by huge rocks that have fallen from impending heights, where, if the traveler should chance to be caught in a freshet, inevitable destruction would be the consequence.[23]

During the summer of 1852 Emory's field parties struggled to complete the survey of the river. Lieutenant Nathaniel Michler, whose operations involved extremely difficult stretches of river, built an observatory at Eagle Pass and worked down to Presidio del Norte. A second party under draftsman Mauritz von Hipple examined the river around the Big Bend toward the mouth of the Pecos River. Beset by the dirt-poor residents of Presidio, whom he considered ". . . the most expert horse thieves in Mexico," von Hipple had to protect his herds while carrying out his assignment.[24] North of Paso, Charles Radziminski, a Polish-born former dragoon officer, led yet another small party between the densely covered banks of the twisting, turning river. On mornings "hot as that place intended for the evil spirits," he and his men slashed their way upstream through the brush from El Paso to Fort Fillmore.[25] Somehow, despite the heat, horse thieves, and the terrain, the work on the long stretch of river was completed. In September, 1852, just before receiving word of the impoundment of the commission's funds, Emory informed Colonel Abert that his men had surveyed the entire Rio Grande from Paso to Laredo.[26]

Resumed under General Robert B. Campbell in the summer of 1853, work proceeded speedily and smoothly. A South Carolinian who won his title as commander of the state militia during the nullification crisis of 1833, Campbell gave Emory a free hand in running the operation. Though one man drowned in the Rio Grande during July, and several came down with yellow fever, the survey continued. Finally, on 10 January 1854, Emory reported that all the fieldwork except the disputed portion from Paso to the mouth of the Gila was finished and that his personnel had arrived in Washington.[27]

While Campbell and Emory completed the survey of the Texan portion of the boundary, the State Department negotiated a second treaty with Mexico. This important compact gave the United States 30,000 square miles of Mexican territory for $10 million. Two southerners, both ex-soldiers, were largely responsible for the acquisition. One was Secretary of War Jefferson Davis, a West Pointer and Mexican War hero, who was the strong man in the cabinet of President Franklin Pierce. The other, Davis's choice to be minister to Mexico, was James Gadsden, formerly an officer in the Corps of Engineers. As president of the South Carolina Railroad Company, Gadsden had championed construction of a transcontinental line with Charleston as the eastern terminus—a plan Davis heartily endorsed. The Gadsden Purchase Treaty, ratified in 1854, placed the coveted right-of-way north of the border and settled the long-standing question of the boundary westward across New Mexico.[28]

The Gadsden settlement achieved several of Emory's long-standing goals. He knew the Gila would not form a satisfactory boundary and desired the inclusion of the area south of the river as the best route for either a wagon road or a railway to San Diego. Moreover, he believed that a border that ran north along the Rio Grande from El Paso del Norte, instead of crossing the river at the town, would be difficult to defend since American troops would not have access to the mountain passes west of the river.[29]

Serving as United States Commissioner, Emory finished the survey of the Gadsden Purchase line in 1854–1855. He and Mexican Commissioner Ylarrigui José Salazar worked smoothly together, while Emory's experienced subordinates swiftly and efficiently completed the fieldwork. Lieutenant Michler worked eastward from the mouth of the Gila, while Emory and topog Lieutenant Charles N. Turnbull went westward from Paso. In just over a year the survey was finished, and Emory and Salazar signed an agreement expressing their satisfaction with the line.[30] After six years the boundary was finally complete.

Through the many personal squabbles and political disputes which attended the lengthy project, the topogs provided the talent and continuity that kept the survey going. With the notable exception of Colonel Graham, officers of the Topographical Engineers avoided the bickering that marred the enterprise.[31] Whipple, Michler, and Emory worked diligently and doggedly, even when all seemed to collapse around them. Emory also performed an exceptional political feat, opposing the initial boundary while managing to avoid involvement in the battles that broke out over it. And, all the while, he kept the work going. The final result was in large measure a monument to this strong-willed and able officer.

In addition to determining the boundary with Mexico, the survey achieved significant and enduring scientific results. The scientists and collectors who accompanied the numerous field parties accumulated a remarkable amount of data and great quantities of natural history specimens. These collectors and their colleagues in the East, who analyzed the data for publication, made substantial contributions to scientific knowledge of the borderlands. Some of the greatest men in American science participated in the collection, organization, and publication of the Commission's field acquisitions. Louis Agassiz, John Torrey, James Hall, and the Smithsonian's Joseph Henry and Spencer Baird all lent their talents to the project.

Throughout the entire period of the survey, Emory corresponded regularly with Baird on the organization of the scientific endeavor. Always interested in government explorations, Baird assisted Emory in selecting personnel and in arranging for the safe delivery of specimens from the border. He also encouraged the effort with appeals to Emory's greatest weakness, his vanity. Repeatedly Baird warned that other collectors in the Southwest might publish the results of their findings first and diminish the significance of Emory's work if specimens were not quickly packed and sent east. But as shrewd and experienced as he was, even Baird could not suppress his astonishment at the number of new species. He was particularly surprised and delighted at the vast collections assembled in a short time by his former student at Dickinson College, John F. Clark. In only three months, Clark sent Baird 125 different species of fish and reptiles, most of them new to science. More surprising still, Clark was a botanist and accumulated these zoological specimens in his spare time![32] "The entire annals of zoological history," Baird wrote Emory, "scarcely presents a parallel to this case."[33]

Emory understood the opportunity that government explorations presented to the nation's scientists. He told the 1851 meeting of the American Association for the Advancement of Science that "the importance of scientific works, undertaken by the government, as exponents of the state of science in the country at any particular period, cannot be overrated, and men of science are therefore interested, and should be consulted in regard to the organization of such works."[34] The Boundary Commission gave interested scholars a rare opportunity to study the fauna, flora, and minerals of the Southwest, and those who were asked to participate responded with interest and energy. The distinguished Columbia University scientist John Torrey assessed most of the botanical specimens, while George Engelmann, a St. Louis physician and an expert botanist, examined the cacti. Professor James Hall evaluated geological specimens delivered to him at his Albany home. Baird himself worked on the fishes and reptiles. This cooperative effort made Emory's report of the survey into an encyclopedia of borderlands natural history.

Scientists also disseminated the new discoveries through the European scholarly community. Engelmann sent a complete set of duplicate cacti specimens to the Cambridge Botanical Garden in England and samples to European collectors. Torrey also gave some of his botanical specimens to his friend Eugene Delaire, head gardener at the Orléans, France, botanical garden.[35] Thus, American scholars shared the excitement of the new discoveries with scientists across the Atlantic. Engelmann spoke for all the rest when he thanked Emory for "the interest you continue to take in natural science."[36]

Employment on the boundary survey and other government expeditions of the same period was of great importance to many young scientists. Geologist Charles Parry, for example, was Torrey's student when his mentor found him a position with Emory. Later Colorado's foremost pioneer botanist, Parry gained valuable experience in collecting with the Commission. Engineer explorations amounted to a graduate school for young naturalists.[37] The old mountainmen had shown the Engineers the geographic secrets of the West. Now, as the process of exploration continued, Corps expeditions gave a generation of budding scientists the opportunity to discover other mysteries and to mature professionally.

Emory's report of the boundary survey, published in 1857, was his last contribution to geographic knowledge, and his greatest. Undistinguished as literature, it was a scientific triumph. Thorough, precise, and admirably illustrated, it gave a faithful picture of the borderlands. Its three thick quarto volumes contained accounts of the survey, detailed descriptions of the country, and field reports on geology, botany, and zoology, together with the findings of the leading scientists who classified the specimens. Accompanying the report was a master map, drawn to a scale of 1:6,000,000, of the entire trans-Mississippi West. Welcomed by scholars here and abroad, these results of the boundary survey, were, as historian William H. Goetzmann observed, "the brightest lights in that sombre adventure along the Rio Grande."[38]

Although publication of the report marked the end of the Mexican boundary survey, the Topographical Engineers began work on a similar assignment far to the north. In 1857 they started work on the first phase of the Canadian boundary survey west of Lake of the Woods. The project was carried out in two parts. During 1857–1861, surveyors marked the line between the Strait of Juan de Fuca and the summit of the Rocky Mountains. Eleven years later a second joint commission started to run the boundary from Lake of the Woods to the Rockies. The 1,300-mile border along the forty-ninth parallel, finished in 1875, was the longest international boundary formed by a continuous curve.

The demarcation of the border from the crest of the Rockies to the Pacific coast was required by the Buchanan-Pakenham Treaty of 1846, which ended the joint occupation of the Oregon country. Peacefully negotiated and still untroubled by Indian raids, the northwestern boundary was a less urgent project than the just-completed Mexican survey. There were resemblances: both combined geodesy with cartography and natural history, and both were conducted by international commissions, but the Canadian survey progressed in a more tranquil atmosphere, without the political conflicts and personal animosities that plagued the earlier effort. One diplomatic dispute arose

Marking the boundary west of Lake of the Woods.

The harsh northern climate and heavily wooded terrain severely limited the amount that could be done in a season. Lieutenant John G. Parke of the Topographical Engineers, the American commission's chief astronomer and surveyor, slogged through foot-deep snow in the summer of 1859 as he moved east from the Skagit River to the Columbia. In the Similkameen and Okinakane valleys, Parke had to wait for axmen to clear a path through the fir and pine forest before he could proceed. This was was not an uncommon problem. Commissioner Campbell estimated that trails had to be opened for three-fourths of the distance traveled. In addition, the Frazer River gold rush caused confusion, postponement, and expense as the prices of supplies and labor skyrocketed. In spite of these difficulties, field operations progressed smoothly until their completion early in 1861.[41]

The commission's work in natural history was carried out on a smaller scale than during the Mexican survey. Naturalist C. B. R. Kennerly and geologist George Gibbs were the only scientists to accompany the field parties. They forwarded their collections to Washington for examination by specialists, among whom were John Newberry, Elliot Coues, and John Torrey. The effort went for naught, however, since the Civil War interrupted the office work of the commission and no report was ever published.[42]

On the second phase of the survey, from the Rockies east to Lake of the Woods, four Engineer officers assisted United States Commissioner Campbell. Major Francis U. Farquhar began as chief astronomer in 1872, but was reassigned in the following year. His replacement, Captain William J. Twining, completed the work with the assistance of Lieutenant James F. Gregory. The fourth Engineer, Lieutenant Francis V. Greene, supervised the tracing of the boundary line and the topographical work. One of Twining's British counterparts was Lieutenant Albany Featherstonhaugh of the Royal Engineers, whose geologist father had once worked for the Topographical Bureau.[43]

The British surveyors' reluctance to commit themselves regarding the starting point of the survey at Lake of the Woods caused some delay and annoyance. Foreign Office efforts were then underway to convince the United States to give up the northwest angle of the lake. This small peninsula which jutted eastward into the water and was not contiguous to the United States had been surrendered by Britain as part of the Webster-Ashburton Treaty of 1842. Tension over this matter caused some ill-feeling between the two parties. But after diplomatic efforts to obtain the peninsula failed, the British commission assumed a more cooperative attitude.[44]

Throughout the period of the survey, field parties fortunately avoided major Indian fights. The northern plains tribes were increasingly hostile in the early part of the decade. Piegan warriors raided British parties twice, but the Americans experienced no troubles. Lieutenant Greene, who later rose to prominence as a soldier, historian, and police

The camp of the boundary commission, December 1873.

commissioner of New York City, surmised in 1874 that Lieutenant Colonel George A. Custer's Black Hills Expedition inadvertantly protected the boundary commission. With the potentially belligerent Sioux lured away from the scene of operations by Custer's activities, the only Indians Greene saw were curious, not hostile.[45]

An Ojibway camp near Lake of the Woods.

The fieldwork on the 900-mile portion of the line was finished in 1875. A meeting of the two nations' representatives in London during the following spring concluded operations along the Canadian border.[46] The London meeting also marked the end of a long and complicated chapter in the history of the Corps of Engineers. From 1849, when Major Emory began work on the Mexican boundary, until Lieutenant Greene's departure from the field in 1875, Engineer officers provided the leadership and technical skill necessary to bring both surveys to successful conclusions. They faced and overcame numerous obstacles, from difficult terrain and hostile Indians to partisan political feuds, to complete the basic boundaries that still separate the forty-eight contiguous states from Canada and Mexico.

Notes

1. Treaty with the Republic of Mexico, 2 February 1848, Art. V, 9 *Stat.* 926; Edward S. Wallace, *The Great Reconnaissance, Soldiers, Artists, and Scientists on the Frontier 1848-1861* (Boston: Little, Brown, 1955), p. 26; Warren, *Memoir*, p., 84.
2. John D. Wade, "John Disturnell," *Dictionary of American Biography*, V (New York: Charles Scribner's Sons, 1943), p. 319.
3. Ralph P. Bieber and Averam B. Bender, eds., *Exploring Southwestern Trails 1846-1854 by Philip St. George Cooke, William Henry Chase Whiting, François Xavier Aubrey* (Glendale, Calif.: Arthur H. Clarke, 1938), p. 310.
4. Colonel John J. Abert to Major William H. Emory, 29 May 1849, William H. Emory Papers, Yale University.
5. Emory to John B. Weller, 8 July 1849, Emory Papers; Secretary of the Interior, *Report in Relation to the Operations of the Commission Appointed to Run and Mark the Boundary between the United States and Mexico*, 31st Cong., 1st sess., Executive Document 34, pt. 1, p. 31.
6. E. I. Edwards, ed., *The Whipple Report: Journal of an Expedition from San Diego, California, to the Rio Grande, from Sept. 11 to Dec. 11, 1849, by A. W. Whipple* (Los Angeles: Westernlore Press, 1961), pp. 71-72; Secretary of the Interior, *Operations of the Boundary Commission*, p. 33.
7. Edwards, ed., *The Whipple Report*, pp. 81-89.
8. Quoted in Edwards, ed., *The Whipple Report*, p. 12.
9. Whipple to Emory, 10 October 1849, Emory Papers.
10. Quoted in Secretary of the Interior, *Operations of the Boundary Commission*, p. 15.
11. Secretary of the Interior, *Operations of the Boundary Commission*, pp. 9, 11-12, 28; Goetzmann, *Army Exploration*, pp. 163-65, 168-69; Emory to Baron von Gerolt, 11 June 1854, Emory Papers; Benton, *Thirty Years View*, II, pp. 715-16.
12. Goetzmann, *Army Exploration*, p. 170.
13. William H. Emory, *United States and Mexican Boundary Survey, Report of William H. Emory, Major First Cavalry and U. S. Commissioner*, 34th Cong., 1st sess., House of Representatives Executive Document 135, Vol. I, p. 11.
14. Wallace, *The Great Reconnaissance*, pp. 12, 24, 26-28; James D. Graham, *The Report of Lieutenant Colonel Graham on the Subject*

of the Boundary Line Between the United States and Mexico, 32d
Cong., 1st sess., Executive Document 121, pp. 23-33.
15. Graham, *The Boundary Line*, pp. 24-26.
16. Graham, *The Boundary Line*, pp. 48, 144-46, 152-54.
17. *Cong. Globe*, 32d Cong., 1st sess., Vol. 21, pt. 2, pp. 1660-61, and
Appendix, pp. 797-807.
18. Secretary of the Interior A. H. H. Stuart to Emory, 15 September 1851,
Emory Papers; Goetzmann, *Army Exploration*, pp. 178, 186-88,
193-94.
19. Emory to John Torrey, 16 September 1851, Emory Papers.
20. Emory to Joseph Henry, 13 October 1851, Emory Papers.
21. Emory to Colonel Abert, 1 May 1852, Emory Papers; Emory, *United
States and Mexican Boundary Survey*, I, p. 12.
22. Emory to Secretary of State James S. Buchanan, [December] 1848,
Emory Papers.
23. Emory, *United States and Mexican Boundary Survey*, I, p. 11.
24. Mauritz von Hipple to Emory, 15 May 1852, Emory Papers.
25. Charles Radziminski to Emory, 21 May 1852, Emory Papers.
26. Emory to Colonel Abert, 1 March 1852, and 30 September 1852,
Emory Papers.
27. Emory, *United States and Mexican Boundary Survey*, I, p. 16; Emory
to Colonel Abert, 10 January 1854, Emory Papers; Goetzmann, *Army
Exploration*, p. 104.
28. For a comprehensive account of the agreement, see Paul Neff Garber,
The Gadsden Treaty (Gloucester, Mass.: Peter Smith, 1959).
29. James W. Magoffin to Emory, 24 April 1853, and Emory to Colonel
Abert, 11 August 1853, Emory Papers; Wallace, *The Great
Reconnaissance*, pp. 28, 93.
30. Goetzmann, *Army Exploration*, pp. 194-96; Emory, *United States
and Mexican Boundary Survey*, I, pp. 23-25; Emory to Secretary of the
Interior Robert McClelland, 25 September 1855, Emory Papers.
31. Goetzmann, *Army Exploration*, p. 208.
32. Spencer F. Baird to Emory, 3 October 1851, 30 January 1852, 10
January 1853, 9 March and 10 June 1855, Spencer F. Baird Papers,
Smithsonian Institution.
33. Baird to Emory, n. d. [1852], Baird Papers.
34. Unidentified newspaper clipping reporting meeting of American
Association for the Advancement of Science, Cincinnati, July, 1851,
Emory Papers.
35. John Torrey to Emory, 5 May 1852, Emory Papers.
36. George Engelmann to Emory, 7 September 1852, Emory Papers.
37. Joseph A. Ewan, *Rocky Mountain Naturalists* (Denver: University of
Denver, 1950), pp. 34-35; A. Hunter Dupree, *Science in the Federal
Government, A History of Policies and Activities to 1940* (Cambridge:
Harvard University, 1957), p. 94.
38. Goetzmann, *Army Exploration*, p. 208.

39. Marcus Baker, "Survey of the Northwestern Boundary of the United States 1857-1861," United States Geological Survey, *Bulletin 174* (Washington, D.C.: Government Printing Office, 1900), pp. 9, 13.
40. Baker, "Northwestern Boundary," pp. 15-16.
41. Baker, "Northwestern Boundary," pp. 17, 69-70, 76.
42. Baker, "Northwestern Boundary," pp. 61-62; Goetzmann, *Army Exploration*, p. 428.
43. George M. Wheeler, *Report Upon United States Geographical Surveys West of the One Hundredth Meridian*, I (Washington, D.C.: Government Printing Office, 1899), p. 778; John E. Parsons, *West on the 49th Parallel, Red River to the Rockies 1872-1876* (New York: William Morrow, 1963), pp. 19-20, 22, 58.
44. Parsons, *West on the 49th Parallel*, pp. 4, 38-39.
45. Parsons, *West on the 49th Parallel*, pp. 99, 109, 121, 156.
46. Parsons, *West on the 49th Parallel*, pp. 136, 139.

Chapter V

THE SOUTHWESTERN RECONNAISSANCE
1849–1860

A complex mission faced the Topographical Engineers in the territory obtained from Mexico. Numerous expeditions, with assignments tailored to fit the needs of specific locales, went into the Southwest. Some places required basic exploration; others, more settled, needed roads to connect towns and forts. Elsewhere, topogs located sites for military posts and railroad passes, reconnoitered rivers, and improved harbors. From the Grand Canyon to the Great Salt Lake, San Antonio to San Diego, the topogs crossed and recrossed the Southwest, examining the new country and binding it to the old.

In Texas, where the great need was for roads, the San Antonio headquarters of the Army's Department of Texas served as the hub from which exploring parties sought potential routes. Lieutenant Colonel Joseph E. Johnston, a veteran of the Seminole and Mexican wars, supervised the effort, and four topogs (Lieutenants Martin L. Smith, William F. Smith, Francis T. Bryan, and Nathaniel Michler), and Lieutenant William H. C. Whiting of the Corps of Engineers undertook the reconnaissances. Unlike the complex scientific surveys of Abert and Emory, the work done under Johnston was practical and grindingly hard. With two potential enemies, Mexico across the Rio Grande and numerous bands of hostile Indians on both sides of the river, Texas desperately needed a network of roads between posts along the border and in the interior. From 1849 to 1851, Johnston and his five hard-working assistants overcame many obstacles, from thieving bands of Apaches to the dry tableland between the Concho and Pecos rivers, to lay out a basic system of transportation and communication that tied the forts and towns together.[1]

The last expeditions in Texas before the Civil War, led by topog Lieutenant William H. Echols in 1859 and 1860, were among the most unusual of the entire southwestern reconnaissance. Although his assignment was conventional—examination of western Texas between the Pecos and Fort Davis and survey of a road between Forts Davis and Stockton—his pack animals were not. Echols and his escort carried their supplies and equipment on camelback. On his first assignment after graduation from the Military Academy, Echols was the second officer to conduct an extensive field test of the camels.[2]

Joseph E. Johnston. *National Archives.*

In many ways camels were ideally suited for the arid Southwest. They drank only once every three days, and carried 500-pound loads. Their large, flexible lips took in food without aid of the tongue and thus preserved moisture. But they also had drawbacks. Their stench drove horses crazy, and their frightening growl made them unpopular among the soldiers. A man who loaded a smelly dromedary while the animal groaned and spat its foul, sticky cud, did not soon forget the experience. If he angered the camel, he also had to look to his kneecaps, not just at the moment but for some time thereafter. Camels remembered abuse and sometimes waited for days before finding an opportunity to knock down a soldier, lie on him and crush him, or bite off a kneecap or arm. For all their suitability, the camels were distrusted and disliked by men who worked with them.[3]

Echols's 1860 tour of the arid and extremely rugged Big Bend country provided an excellent test for the camels. On the "roughest, most tortuous and most cragged" trail he had ever seen, Echols and his men suffered immensely for lack of water, and the mules became too weak to move. The camels, on the other hand, stood the torture well and proved just as sure-footed as the mules. Echols's journal is full of praise for the durability and strength of the new pack animals. After one particularly trying day he said simply, "No such march as this could be made with any security without them." The department commander, Brevet Colonel Robert E. Lee, agreed that the camels proved themselves in the Big Bend. Lee praised their "endurance, docility, and sagacity," and attributed the success of the reconnaissance to their "reliable services."[4]

The Echols expeditions ended both the survey of Texas and the camel experiment. The War Department's request for one thousand of the animals found little support in a Congress preoccupied with sectional tensions. When the Civil War started, the Army had 111 camels, 80 in Texas and 31 in California. Neither the camels in Texas, which became Confederate prisoners of war, nor the others received proper care. All of them ultimately found their way into the wilderness where they died off. The country was concerned with more important matters.[5]

Like the Texas reconnaissance, the postwar exploration of New Mexico began in 1849. Captain Randolph B. Marcy, escorting an emigrant caravan from Fort Smith, Arkansas, to Santa Fe, led the first expedition into the territory along the south side of the Canadian River. Lieutenant James H. Simpson, eleven years a topog, rode with Marcy. An unhappy novice in western exploration who was ordered to New Mexico from a pleasant assignment as superintendent of lighthouse construction near Monroe, Michigan, Simpson identified and recorded prominent landmarks to guide later wagon trains. When Marcy turned back toward Texas, Simpson stayed in New Mexico and reported for duty with Lieutenant Colonel John N. Washington's Ninth Military Department.[6]

Shortly after his arrival, Simpson met topographer Edward (Ned) Kern and his artist brother Richard. The Kerns had a grisly story to tell. Respected naturalists and members of the Philadelphia Academy of Natural Sciences, both were drawn irresistibly by the West. They and their brother Benjamin, a physician, had jumped at the chance to accompany Frémont on a privately financed railroad survey in 1848. As autumn became winter, the invigorating season of fieldwork turned into the grimmest of disasters. Lost, chilled to the bone, and so hungry they tried to trap mice, Frémont and his men stumbled blindly through slashing blizzards in the San Juan Mountains near the headwaters of the Rio Grande. The mules died first, then the men began to succumb. In despair, Frémont relinquished command, and it became every man for himself. The Kerns stuck together and stumbled upon relief in late January. Weak and almost deranged, they wept at the sight of bread and meat. Eleven of their thirty companions never escaped the white horror.[7]

There was still more to the tale. Frémont cast all blame for the disaster on guide Bill Williams, and even accused him of cannibalism: "In starving times," Frémont said, "no man who knew him ever walked in front of Bill Williams."[8] The unfortunate Williams never had the chance to defend himself. In March, 1849, as he and Ben Kern made their way back toward the mountains to recover possessions cached during the winter, a band of Utes surprised and killed both.[9] When Ned and Richard met Simpson, they had little left beside their great talents and sorrowful memories.

Simpson could do nothing to blot out the memories, but he could offer them work. Assigned to guide Colonel Washington's expedition against the Navahoes and survey the country traversed by the column, Simpson hired Ned as topographer and Dick as artist. The Navahoes, called "the Earth People" in their own language and now famous as shepherds and horsemen, silversmiths and weavers, had achieved another kind of renown by the end of the Mexican War. The most feared raiders on the New Mexican plateau, they terrorized white settlements as well as their Zuni and Hopi neighbors.[10] Colonel Washington intended to strike deep into their canyon strongholds and end the tribe's career as the scourge of New Mexican settlements.

Across the continental divide and up the Rio Chaco, Simpson and his assistants rode with Washington and his men, yet barely seemed part of the expedition. In the chasms of the Chaco, they became absorbed in investigating the ruins of ancient Indian pueblos, large prehistoric communities of stone, mortar, and wood, incredibly assembled with only stone tools by unknown builders. In a ten-mile strip of the canyon floor, Simpson found twelve large community houses, each capable of housing several hundred to a thousand residents, as well as many smaller structures. He estimated that one of the larger ones, which he dubbed Chettro Kettle (now written Chetro Ketl), was built of over thirty million pieces of stone, a guess that has been revised to fifty million by modern archaeologists. While Richard Kern sketched and mapped the canyon, Simpson moved delightedly from Chetro Ketl to Pueblo Bonito, then to Pueblo del Arroyo, visiting the accessible rooms, counting, measuring, and describing his discoveries. Finally he had to stop and rejoin the expedition. He still worked for Colonel Washington.[11]

Simpson's discoveries in Chaco Canyon and later in Canyon de Chelly were of lasting scientific importance. In a region then unknown to Anglo-Americans, he found one of the most important archaeological sites in the United States. Accounts of the pueblo cultures still begin with reference to Simpson's discoveries and Kern's drawings. While pushing back the physical frontier, Simpson showed the way to new scientific and cultural horizons.[12]

In contrast to Simpson's successful probe of the canyons, Washington's punitive foray turned into a tragic farce. At a time when Navahoes and Mexicans stole countless mounts from each other, the soldiers killed the aged, rheumatic Navaho chief Narbona for the theft of one horse. After the shooting, the Indians signed the treaty proffered by Washington, but only to make him go away. He succeeded only in adding to the growing hostility of the Navahoes before he and his troops withdrew.[13]

76

Ruins in the Canyon de Chelly.

In September, 1851, Captain Lorenzo Sitgreaves of the Topographical Engineers continued the reconnaissance of New Mexico. Seeking the westward wagon road that Simpson believed feasible from Albuquerque to the Colorado and perhaps all the way to Los Angeles, Sitgreaves, Lieutenant John G. Parke, Richard Kern, and an infantry escort went

The sandstone walls of Canyon de Chelly.

around the San Francisco Mountains and across the great Colorado River to California. With nineteen years of service, thirteen of them in the Topographical Engineers, Sitgreaves made a good teacher for Parke, also a topog but in the West for the first time. Although harrassed by Mohave and Yuma warriors, the party reconnoitered the slightly known country between Canyon de Chelly and the Colorado. Sitgreaves disliked the Southwest even more than Simpson and, in his twenty-page report, summed up the 250-mile expanse between Bill Williams Mountain and San Diego in a single sentence: "The whole country traversed from the San Francisco mountains was barren and devoid of interest."[14]

Three Mohave Indians.

After Sitgreaves's expedition came a period of road surveys and construction. In 1854, Congress voted appropriations for improvement of territorial roads, some cut by arroyos and others scarcely more than bridle paths, but all little better than the open country they crossed. Captain Eliakim P. Scammon of the Topographical Engineers, once an assistant in the preparation of Nicollet's map of the Mississippi drainage system, took charge of the work. During two years in Santa Fe, Scammon spent most of the money but made very little progress on the roads. Unschooled in road building and bewildered by the complexities of the bookkeeping, Scammon was finally dismissed from the service for failure to account properly for $350 in public funds. When Captain John N. Macomb took over in 1856, the work began in earnest.[15]

Almost halfway through a military career that spanned fifty years, Macomb wasted no time getting started. After surveying the potential routes, he hired civilian crews for the actual construction. Normally, this involved merely grading and widening paths for use by wagons. Some of the roads required more extensive improvement, and Macomb's work crews bridged gullies, paved steep grades with finely crushed rock (called macadam after the developer of the technique, Scottish engineer John L. McAdam), and erected dry masonry walls to shield the exposed sides of mountain roads from flash floods. By the time he was transferred in 1859, Macomb completed several major routes. Together with trails examined by earlier explorers, the Macomb roads formed the basis for New Mexico's highway and railroad system.[16]

The view from Captain Sitgreaves' camp on the Colorado.

Establishment of communications with California was the object of much of the work topogs did in Texas and New Mexico after the Mexican War. The 1848 discovery of gold in the American River triggered a wave of emigration to the new Golconda. While many gold-seekers found their way across the central plains and the Great Basin with the help of Fremont's map, others crossed the Southwest with Emory's map in hand. Emory and Amiel Whipple, at work on the Mexican boundary in 1849, saw many parties, some suffering terribly, along the southern route. The commander of the Tenth Military Department authorized Emory to give supplies to the needy and directed him to locate a military post at the junction of the Gila and Colorado rivers. Known first as Camp Yuma and later given permanent status as a fort, Yuma protected travelers along the trail to California throughout the gold rush years.[17]

Yuma was the very definition of an isolated frontier outpost. In the

79

middle of a parched wasteland populated by unfriendly Indians, where the mean December temperature was a blistering 92°F, the camp seemed more a place of banishment than an ordinary post. Some claimed hens laid hard-boiled eggs there. Lieutenant George H. Derby, a topog assigned in 1850 to ascertain the navigability of the Colorado up to Yuma, said a villainous soldier who died there and went straight to hell telegraphed back for his blankets.[18] Later, in one of his humorous essays on astronomy, published under the pseudonym John Phoenix, Derby compared the relative desirability of establishing posts at Yuma and on the planet Mercury:

> [Mercury] receives six and a half times as much heat from the sun as we do; from which we conclude that the climate must be very similar to that of Fort Yuma, on the Colorado River. The difficulty of communication with Mercury will probably prevent its ever being selected as a military post, though it possesses many advantages for that purpose, being extremely inaccessible, inconvenient, and doubtless, singularly uncomfortable.[19]

"The Ass-sault," a tactical innovation by John Phoenix. When the recoiling artillery drove the mule forward, it would respond by charging backward—toward the enemy.

Hoping to reduce the tremendous expense and uncertainty of supplying the post overland from San Diego, the Army sent Derby up the Colorado aboard an ocean-going schooner. Although he was a capable veteran of the Mexican War, the Missouri River frontier, and the California goldfields, Derby was primarily known for his humor. Even during his years at West Point, among his classmates George B. McClellan and Thomas "Stonewall" Jackson, he had been irrepressible. When, for example, a professor asked him the proper course of action as commander of a beseiged fort sure to fall in forty-five days, Derby replied, "I would march out, let the enemy in, and at the end of forty-five days, I would change places with him."[20] Matching his brash wit with solid ability, Derby completed his reconnaissance of the Colorado from its mouth at Guyamas on the Gulf of California to Yuma. Thereafter, the small post astraddle the southern emigrant road to California was assured of regular provisions.[21]

George H. Derby. *National Archives.*

81

Three Topographical Engineers, Captain William H. Warner and Lieutenants Robert S. Williamson and Derby, performed a variety of tasks in California. Warner, Chief Topographical Engineer of the Tenth Military Department after recovering from wounds sustained at San Pasqual, began his work in 1847. He made extensive examinations of routes connecting San Diego and San Francisco before leading an expedition east into the Sierra Nevada with Lieutenant Williamson.

In August, 1849, Warner and Williamson left Sacramento in quest of a railroad route through the mountains to the Great Basin. Guided by François Berçier, an old voyageur for the Hudson's Bay Company, and accompanied by eleven civilian assistants they rode northward up the Sacramento toward the country of the Klamaths, who four years previously had attacked Frémont and killed several of his men. Warner left Williamson and most of his infantry escort near Deer Creek Pass and followed the Pit River to its source near Goose Lake in the northeastern corner of California, where he found his railroad pass.[22]

When he and Williamson reached the eastern edge of the mountains the great surge of Argonauts was about to descend on California. Several gold-seekers, coming over the mountains on the Lassen Trail, told the surprised topogs that ten or twenty thousand more were behind them. The flood, which had already swept over the Platte River road, would soon inundate California. The gold rush was on.

Warner and his party were making their way back toward Sacramento along Frémont's 1844 route when disaster struck. On September 26, as he and Bercier nudged their mounts up a steep hill, Pit River Indians surprised and killed them. Lieutenant Williamson filed this report:

> ... a party of about twenty-five Indians, who had been lying in ambush behind some large rocks near the summit, suddenly sprang up and shot a volley of arrows into the party. The greater number of the arrows took effect upon the Captain and the guide, and both were mortally wounded. The Captain's mule turned with him, and plunged down the hill; and having been carried about two hundred yards, he fell from the animal dead.[23]

Williamson managed to recover Warner's notebooks before he withdrew to Sacramento to compile a report and map.

Not all topog assignments in California ended in such tragedy. In 1853, when silt from the San Diego River threatened to ruin San Diego's fine harbor, Lieutenant Derby left a staff job in San Francisco to supervise improvement of the channel. He departed from the Golden Gate in typical Derby style. At dinner in a hotel before he left, he watched the innkeeper carving a roast of veal into small pieces, because, as his host explained, "there is but little of it, and I want to make it go as far as possible." "In that case," Derby replied, "I'll take a large piece. I think I can make it go as far as anybody; I am going to San Diego."[24]

At San Diego, or Sandyago as he sometimes spelled it, Derby the topog took a backseat to his alter ego, humorist John Phoenix. While the topog worked on the diversion of the river, the humorist had a field day writing for the San Diego *Herald*, which the editor once turned over to him for two weeks. When work on the harbor proved frustrating, Phoenix told his readers that Derby "was sent out from Washington ... 'to dam the San Diego River,' and he informed me with a deep sigh and melancholy smile that he had done it (mentally) several times since his arrival." Always dedicated to keeping his readers abreast of engineering developments, Phoenix issued the following statement: "The report that Lieutenant Derby has sent to San Francisco for a lathe, to be used in turning the San Diego River is, we understand, entirely without foundation."[25] When Derby and Phoenix left San Diego in 1855, they left not only an incomplete dam that was partially washed away by a storm the following year, but also an enduring contribution to American humor.

While Warner, Williamson, and Derby toiled in California, other topogs worked in the Great Basin. Two major expeditions probed the region during the years following the Mexican War. Captain Howard Stansbury, commissioned in 1838 after more than a decade as a civil engineer for the Topographical Bureau, led the first reconnaissance. His assistant, Lieutenant John W. Gunnison, entered the service in 1837 after graduating near the top of his West Point class. Neither had any experience in western exploration, when, on the last day of May, 1849, they left Fort Leavenworth to explore the Great Salt Lake and its valley.

In mid-October Stansbury, Gunnison, and a small band of hardy mountaineers stood on the shore of the lake, preparing for their journey around the inland sea. The old-timers warned against the trip. It was nearly impossible in any season, they said, but the oncoming winter would make the trek even harder. And the Shoshones north of the lake, still mourning the men murdered while trying to defend their women from assault by California-bound whites, might dispatch those explorers not killed by the brutal march. The time seemed wrong. Nevertheless, on October 19, Stansbury set out on the difficult mission.[26]

Although the trip would take over two weeks and exact its toll in hardship and suffering, Stansbury approached the lake eagerly. He marvelled at the "clear and calm" waters that "stretched far to the south and west," but was even more impressed with the exotic qualities of the vista:

> ... the dreamy haze hovering over this still and solitary sea threw its dim, uncertain veil over the more distant features of the landscape, preventing the eye from discerning any one object with distinctness, while it half revealed the whole, leaving ample scope for the imagination of the beholder. The stillness of the grave seemed to pervade both air and water, and excepting here and there a solitary wild duck floating motionless on the bosom of the lake, not a living thing was to be seen.[27]

After the wonder and awe came torment and pain. Several times the party went entire days without water. In addition, the plain to the north and west of the lake proved extremely difficult to cross. The first part of the route passed over an expanse of dried mud, sparkling with salt crystals. For a while Stansbury's mules crossed the salt flats as they would a sheet of ice. Then rain turned the firm crust into a nearly impassable mire and made travel extremely difficult.[28]

Captain Stansbury completed the reconnaissance on November 7, when he returned to Salt Lake City. Proud of his achievement, he boasted that his detachment was "the first party of white men that ever succeeded in making the entire circuit of the lake by land." He described the region bordering the lake as "an immense level plain, consisting of soft mud, frequently traversed by small meandering rills of salt and sulphurous water, with occasional springs of fresh, all of which sink before reaching the lake."[29]

Snow began to fall as winter set in and made further work impossible. Stansbury established his cantonment in Salt Lake City, and passed the cold months learning about the Latter-Day Saints. He devoted a large portion of his report to a discussion of the development of the Mormon community, which he found to be "a quiet, orderly, industrious, and well-organized society...."[30]

Gunnison included his observations on the Mormons in a book entitled *The Mormons, Or Latter-Day Saints in the Valley of the Great Salt Lake.* He told his inquisitive countrymen a great deal about the community, explaining land use and education as well as the controversial practice of plural marriages. He praised what he found praiseworthy and criticized what he considered distasteful. He was, for example, impressed with the free, well-attended public schools but appalled by the profane language of children on the streets. At a time when discussion of the Mormons generated great passions, both Gunnison and Stansbury took unusually calm and fair positions.[31]

When the topogs resumed active operations in the spring, Captain Stansbury decided to supplement his trip around the lake with an exploration by water. His men built a small wooden sailboat, which they named *Salicornia,* or Flower of Salt Lake, but which soon came to be known as the *Sally.* They spent parts of two months on the water, accumulating data for their map. Stansbury was deeply affected by the vastness and the deathlike quiet of the lake. He recorded his impressions of a solitary night at the helm while his crew slept:

> I shall never forget this night. The silence of the grave was around us, unrelieved by the slightest sound. Not the leaping of a fish nor the solitary cry of a bird was to be heard, as, in profound darkness, the boat moved on, plunging her bow into the black and sullen waters.... The sense of isolation from everything living was painfully oppressive. Even the chirp of a cricket would have formed some link with the world of life; but all was stillness and solitary desolation.[32]

In August Stansbury and Gunnison left Salt Lake City for the return trip to Fort Leavenworth. Their trail over the Green River and then across

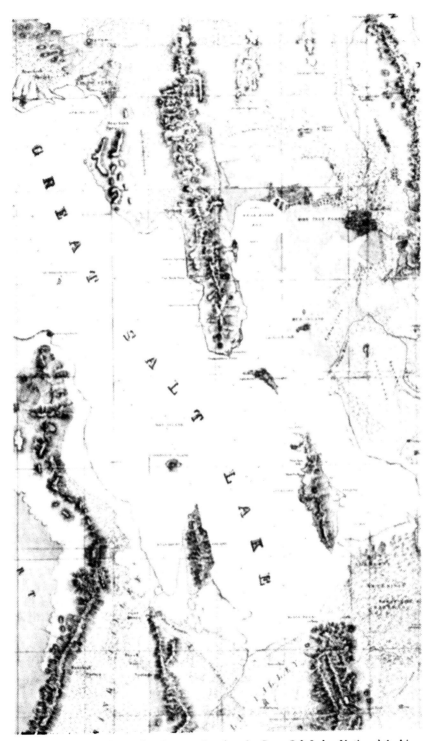

A portion of Howard Stansbury's map, showing the Great Salt Lake. *National Archives.*

the Laramie Plains and along Lodge Pole Creek to its mouth in the South Platte proved to be the shortest and easiest path from Salt Lake City. The discovery of this route, parts of which were later used by the Pony Express and the Union Pacific Railroad, capped a successful expedition, in which Stansbury became the first to travel around the Great Salt Lake and recognize the Great Basin as a prehistoric lakebed. In addition to his major topographical achievements—his successor in the Basin, Captain Simpson, said "it has been a gratification to me to find that [Stansbury's] report and map have represented the country so correctly and have been of much service to me...."—Stansbury accumulated a collection of natural history specimens so large that Spencer Baird of the Smithsonian was prompted to claim that "no government expedition since the days of Major Long's visit to the Missouri has ever presented such important additions to natural history...."[33] His report, published commercially in the United States, England, and Germany, became widely popular in its own time and remains a frontier classic.[34]

Some important questions still awaited resolution after the Stansbury-Gunnison expedition. Simpson went into the basin ten years later to find a wagon road through Utah and Nevada, from Camp Floyd at the south end of the Great Salt Lake to Genoa east of Lake Tahoe in the Carson River valley. Earlier explorers had established routes through the northern basin, most notably along the Humboldt, and other routes skirted the region to the south. Simpson found two paths through the center of the arid country that reduced the trek to California by over two hundred miles. His routes were almost immediately put into use by the Pony Express and the Placerville and St. Joseph Telegraph Company.[35]

While Simpson completed the difficult journey across the Great Basin, other topogs toiled in equally forbidding country to the south. The Colorado River, explored as far as Yuma by Derby, was still largely unknown. Two expeditions, the first led by Lieutenant Joseph C. Ives in 1857 and the second two years later under Captain Macomb, examined the upper reaches of the great river, its tributaries, and the fantastic canyonlands.

The Ives party came to the Colorado to determine its navigability upstream from Yuma. Ives's men brought a fifty-foot-long iron steamer to the mouth of the river in sections and assembled it before a curious crowd of Indians. After mounting a small howitzer at the bow, members of the party gave the boat a coat of paint and printed "Explorer" boldly across the wheelhouse. The boiler was tested successfully on Christmas day, 1857. Five days later Ives reported that "with a shrill scream from the whistle the 'Explorer' started out into the river, and in a moment was shooting along upon the tide with a velocity that made the high bank seem to spin as we glided by." So began the expedition which culminated in the first recorded exploration of the floor of the Grand Canyon.[36]

Fed by driftwood scavenged by the crew and co-operative Indians, the *Explorer* chugged upriver. At Fort Yuma Ives picked up the members of his party who had come overland from San Diego, including geologist

John S. Newberry, topographer F. W. Egloffstein, and the German artist Heinrich B. Möllhausen, a novelist later known as the German James Fenimore Cooper. Although Ives learned that the Indians upstream viewed the impending encroachment with alarm, the possibility of hostilities did not diminish his eagerness to put Yuma behind him. He lacked Derby's flair but shared his opinion of the post: "Fort Yuma is not a place to inspire one with regret at leaving."[37]

Ives did not easily escape from Yuma. Two miles upstream the *Explorer* stuck on a sandbar. The entire party toiled for over four hours, unloading the ship and forcing it into deep water. The operation took place in plain sight of Yuma, and Ives ruefully noted that "this sudden check on our progress was affording an evening of great entertainment to those in and out of the garrison."[38]

The unfriendly interest of the Yuma Indians who watched the *Explorer*'s progress after it churned past the Chocolate Mountains, inadvertantly aided Ives. The vessel's inventor and pilot, sharp-eyed A. J. Carroll, quickly grasped the coincidence between their presence and bad stretches of river. Whenever he saw them gathered he slowed the engine in expectation of the sandbar that inevitably followed. Thus guided, Ives went up toward the head of navigation, hoping to find a convenient supply route via the Colorado to Utah. War with the Mormons was already imminent and the provisioning of forts and even an army in the field was vitally important to the War Department. So it was not only in the interest of science that the *Explorer* made its way through the "low purple gateway" into Mohave Canyon.[39]

Once through the canyon and into the country of the Mohaves, Ives found friendlier guides. To his delight, he located two Indians who had guided Lieutenant Whipple on his Pacific railroad survey in 1854. Whipple had once been reviled by an escort officer for his interest in the Indians, but his kindness to the Mohaves Cairook and Ireteba paid great dividends to Ives. Both agreed to go upriver and, although Cairook turned back after two days, Ireteba remained with the expedition all the way to Black Canyon.[40]

Provisions ran out in the Mohave country and the party was forced to adopt the Indian diet of corn, beans, and river water. Ives hated the food and longed for a well-salted soup made with dog or mule meat. Geologist Newberry also loathed the coarse, plain fare which he thought consisted mainly of sand rather than corn and beans. The sand, he complained to fellow scientist Ferdinand Hayden, was everywhere, in his plate, his bed, and his clothes.[41]

Soon the party reached the head of navigation in Black Canyon, where the Colorado abruptly bent to the east. They examined the canyon in a skiff driven by oars and sails and climbed onto the plateau to locate a connection with the Mormon road to Utah. Then they turned back in the steamer and shot the rapids coming out of Black Canyon. Just downstream a runner from Fort Yuma met them with letters, papers, and the welcome news that a packtrain of supplies approached, promising all

The Ives expedition bound for Black Canyon. *Library of Congress.*

a quick change of diet.

Freshly provisioned and well-rested, Ives sent Carroll and the *Explorer* back to Yuma and headed east with two Hualapais Indian guides. A third tribesman who visited the party was lucky to get away alive. The overzealous Möllhausen, fascinated by what he considered to be this Indian's extraordinary ugliness, wanted to take the poor man east—as a zoological specimen pickled in alcohol. Lieutenant Ives overruled Möllhausen, and the party rode eastward on muleback to intersect the Colorado at Grand Canyon.

After they reconnoitered the plateau, the party began the perilous descent to the canyon floor. Under a blazing sun they nudged their mules down a narrow path cut into the cliffs by Indians. As they eased their way down, the men seemed to Ives "very much like a row of insects crawling upon the side of a building. . . ." On a path barely wide enough for a mule and its rider, Ives's mount trod "within three inches of the brink of a sheer gulf a thousand feet deep." Finally they could ride no more. With a steep cliff at one shoulder and the abyss on the other side, Ives's head spun with dizziness. Slowly, very carefully, he dismounted and led his mule down. Others became even giddier, and "were obliged to creep upon their hands and knees, being unable to walk or stand."[42] Their slim trail ended on a broad ledge. Beyond was only a series of footholds cut in cracks and fissures, "a desperate trail, but located with a good deal of skill." With no water for the animals nearer than a series of pools thirty miles away, the party turned back.

After sending three men for water, Ives and fifteen others tried again, this time on foot. They passed the ledge which marked their earlier progress to within fifty feet of the bottom, where a rickety ladder leaning against the canyon wall offered a way to the floor. Topographer

The Colorado River with the eastern edge of the Grand Canyon in the distance.

Egloffstein made his way gingerly down the ladder, which collapsed just as he touched bottom. His companions retrieved him by means of a rope made from the slings of their rifles. Unable to complete the return climb before nightfall, the small exploring party huddled on the trail, "deeper in the bowels of the earth than we had ever been before, surrounded by walls and towers of such imposing dimensions that it would be useless to attempt describing them...."[43] When day broke, they resumed their trek, and returned to camp thirty perilous miles and twenty-four hungry hours after they began the descent.

Ives described the Grand Canyon region as completely worthless. While proudly claiming that his was the first party of whites into the canyon, he confidently asserted that it would also be the last. Geologist Newberry, on the other hand, found the canyonlands far from useless. The exploration

89

gave him the opportunity to see what no scientist before him had viewed, the vast eroded plateau and gigantic gorges of the canyon.[44] Even Ives understood the significance of the opportunity for Newberry and the science of geology:

> This plateau formation has been undisturbed by volcanic action, and the sides of the canyon exhibit all of the series that compose the tablelands of New Mexico, presenting perhaps the most splendid exposure of stratified rock there is in the world.[45]

After the examination of the canyon, the rest was anticlimax. Ives crossed the Painted Desert to the Hopi villages and Fort Defiance. There he bid farewell to his companions, who continued east to Fort Leavenworth. He took a more circuitous route by way of Santa Fe and El Paso to the west coast and a New York-bound steamer.

Ives never saw the Colorado again, but Newberry returned in 1859 with Captain Macomb. They came overland from Santa Fe, tracing the drainage of the San Juan River, then riding through the canyon country north of the intersection of the Green and Grand rivers. Macomb shared Ives's opinion of the canyonlands: "I cannot conceive of a more worthless and impracticable region than the one we now found ourselves in."[46] Indeed, for almost five hundred miles, the Colorado flowed 3,000 to 6,000 feet below the "abrupt, frequently perpendicular crags and precipices" of the plateau above. Newberry called the region "valueless to the agriculturist; feared and shunned by the emigrant, the miner, and even the adventurous trapper...." But he acknowledged that for him the plateau was a "paradise" because "nowhere on the earth's surface, so far as we know, are the secrets of its structure so fully revealed as here."[47]

Macomb and a small detachment escorted Newberry down to the river from a base camp at Ojo Verde. On their descent they passed through country "everywhere deeply cut by a tangled mass of canyons, and thickly set with towers, castles, and spires, of most varied and striking forms; the most wonderful monuments of erosion which our eyes, already experienced in objects of this kind, had beheld." Grasping for something familiar with which to compare the marvels, Newberry asked readers to imagine "the island of New York thickly set with spires like that of Trinity Church, but many of them full twice its height."[48]

The scientist did not go into the canyon just to indulge in literary flights. His close observations of the walls enabled him to characterize the entire area, where his predecessors had merely catalogued geological features. His work called attention to the value of careful analyses of single mountain ranges or peaks, known as key studies, as a way to understand the basic principles of a region's creation. Geographically and geologically Newberry and Macomb revealed a new and unknown region to their countrymen.[49]

Years before John Wesley Powell's epic journey downsteam from the upper reaches of the Green through the Grand Canyon in 1869, the combined efforts of Derby, Ives, and Macomb gave the nation a substantial amount of information about the Colorado. Newberry in particular made significant geological contributions. Topographer Egloffstein, who descended the rickety ladder to the Grand Canyon floor, accurately depicted the region in a contour map of his own design, which made the mountains stand out in sharp relief.[50] While navigating the river and probing the fantastic chasms of one of American's spectacular wonderlands, the engineer parties made significant contributions to the development of science.

The southwestern reconnaissance served the national concern with the conquest of the continent extremely well. The explorations and road surveys yielded important practical results, among them roads, railroad passes, and telegraph routes. Improvement of harbors, location of forts, and guidance of Indian expeditions offered other utilitarian services. Whether hard and dull like the Texas road surveys, or exciting and exotic like Ives's descent of the Grand Canyon, the expeditions brought back indispensable data on resources, climate, and topography.

While easing the way for the physical growth of the nation, the southwestern reconnaissance of the Topographical Engineers had significant scientific consequences. Simpson's archaeological discoveries, Newberry's geological work, and Stansbury's analysis of the Great Basin's origins all contributed to a deeper comprehension of the nature of the continent. These insights into the human and natural history of North America, combined with the diverse practical contributions to westward expansion, highlighted the time as the heyday of the topogs, their busiest and most fruitful period.

Notes

1. Goetzmann, *Exploration and Empire*, p. 273; Averam B. Bender, "Opening Routes Across West Texas, 1848-1850," *Southwestern Historical Quarterly*, 37 (October 1933), 116, 119, 135.
2. Goetzmann, *Army Exploration*, pp. 363-64; W. Turrentine Jackson, *Wagon Roads West: A Study of Federal Road Surveys and Construction in the Trans-Mississippi West, 1846-1869* (New Haven: Yale University Press, 1965), p. 244; H. W. Caygill, "The Camelization of the Army," *The Military Engineer*, 26 (July-August 1934), 271.
3. Odie B. Faulk, *The U. S. Camel Corps, An Army Experiment* (New York: Oxford University Press, 1976), pp. 20-22, 70-71, 86-87.
4. William H. Echols, *Diary of a Reconnaissance of the Country Between the El Paso Road and the Rio Grande River*, 36th Cong., 2d sess., Senate Executive Document 1, pp. 33, 40.
5. John Shapard, "The United States Army Camel Corps: 1856-1866," *Military Review*, 55 (August 1975), 85-88.
6. Warren, *Memoir*, p. 56; Jackson, *Wagon Roads West*, pp. 25-26; Goetzmann, *Army Exploration*, pp. 213, 217.
7. Robert V. Hine, *Edward Kern and American Expansion* (New Haven: Yale University Press, 1962), pp. 49-50, 58-61, 70-71.
8. Quoted in Hine, *Edward Kern*, p. 62.
9. Hine, *Edward Kern*, pp. 65-66.
10. Ruth M. Underhill, *The Navajos* (Norman: University of Oklahoma Press, 1971), pp. lx, 3, 74.
11. Edgar L. Hewitt, *Ancient Life in the American Southwest* (Indianapolis: Bobbs-Merrill, 1930), pp. 289-93; Frank McNitt, ed., *Navaho Expedition: Journal of a Military Reconnaissance from Santa Fe, New Mexico, to the Navaho Country Made in 1849 by Lieutenant James H. Simpson* (Norman: University of Oklahoma Press, 1954), pp. 3, 43-45.
12. Hewitt, *Ancient Life*, pp. 293, 301; John C. McGregor, *Southwestern Archaeology* (Urbana: University of Illinois Press, 1965), p. 39; Goetzmann, *Army Exploration*, pp. 240, 243-44.
13. Hine, *Edward Kern*, p. 77; Underhill, *The Navajos*, pp. 90, 96-100.
14. Lorenzo Sitgreaves, *Report of an Expedition Down the Zuni and Colorado Rivers*, 32d Cong., 2d sess., Senate Executive Document 59, p. 17.
15. Jackson, *Wagon Roads West*, pp. 107-11, 345.
16. Jackson, *Wagon Roads West*, pp. 112-16, 119, 328.
17. Assistant Adjutant General, Tenth Military Department, to Lieutenant William H. Emory, 26 September 1849, and Lieutenant Cave J. Couts to Emory, 17 October 1849, Emory Papers, Yale University; Odie B. Faulk, ed., *Derby's Report on Opening the*

Colorado, 1850–1851 (Albuquerque: University of New Mexico Press, 1967), pp. 7–8.

18. George R. Stewart, *John Phoenix, Esq., The Veritable Squibob: A Life of Captain George H. Derby, U.S.A.* (New York: Henry Holt, 1937), p. 71.

19. John Phoenix, *Phoenixiana; or, Sketches and Burlesques* (New York: A. Appleton, 1866), p. 59. Also see Phoenix, *The Squibob Papers* (New York: Carleton, 1865).

20. Stewart, *John Phoenix*, p. 38.

21. Faulk, *Derby's Report*, pp. 8–9, 13, 25, 28, 47.

22. Warren, *Memoir*, p. 55; Robert S. Williamson, *Report of the Reconnaissance made by the Late Brevet Captain W. H. Warner of a Route Through the Sierra Nevades by the Upper Sacramento*, 31st Cong., 1st sess., Senate Executive Document 47, pp. 17–20.

23. Williamson, *A Route Through the Sierra Nevadas*, p. 20.

24. Stewart, *John Phoenix*, p. 117.

25. Stewart, *John Phoenix*, pp. 136–37.

26. Howard Stansbury, *Exploration and Survey of the Valley of the Great Salt Lake of Utah, Including a Reconnaissance of a New Route Through the Rocky Mountains*, 32d Cong., Special sess., Senate Executive Document 3, pp. 13, 97–98. The following account of Stansbury's expedition is based on this report. Footnotes are provided only for portions quoted in the text.

27. Stansbury, *The Valley of the Great Salt Lake*, p. 101.

28. Stansbury, *The Valley of the Great Salt Lake*, p. 111.

29. Stansbury, *The Valley of the Great Salt Lake*, pp. 118–19.

30. Stansbury, *The Valley of the Great Salt Lake*, p. 134.

31. Andrew Love Neff, *History of Utah 1847 to 1869*, ed. by Leland H. Creer (Salt Lake City: The Deseret News Press, 1940), pp. 264, 354, 558, 605; Goetzmann, *Army Exploration*, pp. 222–23.

32. Stansbury, *The Valley of the Great Salt Lake*, pp. 187–88.

33. James H. Simpson, *Report of Explorations Across the Great Basin of the Territory of Utah For a Direct Wagon-Route From Camp Floyd to Genoa, in Carson Valley in 1859* (Washington: Government Printing Office, 1876), p. 23; Goetzmann, *Army Exploration*, p. 224.

34. Goetzmann, *Army Exploration*, p. 224.

35. Simpson, *Across the Great Basin*, pp. 25–26; McNitt, ed., *Navaho Expedition*, p. 237.

36. Joseph C. Ives, *Report Upon the Colorado River of the West*, 36th Cong., 1st sess., Executive Document, pp. 21, 38. Unless otherwise indicated, the following account of the Ives expedition is based on this report. Footnotes are provided only for portions quoted in the text.

37. Ives, *Colorado River of the West*, p. 43.

38. Ives, *Colorado River of the West*, p. 46.

39. Ives, *Colorado River of the West*, p. 63; Goetzmann, *Army Exploration*, pp. 375, 381–82.

40. Edwards, ed., *The Whipple Report*, p. 13.
41. Merrill, *First One Hundred Years of American Geology*, p. 684.
42. Ives, *Colorado River of the West*, p. 106.
43. Ives, *Colorado River of the West*, p. 107.
44. Goetzmann, *Exploration and Empire*, p. 308.
45. Ives, *Colorado River of the West*, pp. 100-01.
46. John N. Macomb, *Report of Captain J. N. Macomb, Topographical Engineers, in charge of San Juan Expedition*, 36th Cong., 2d sess., Senate Executive Document 1, pp. 149-50.
47. John S. Newberry, "Geological Report," in Macomb, *Report of the Exploring Expedition from Santa Fe, New Mexico, to the Junction of the Grand and Green Rivers of the Great Colorado of the West, in 1859* (Washington: Government Printing Office, 1876), pp. 54-55; Goetzmann, *Army Exploration*, p. 397.
48. Newberry, "Geological Report," pp. 93-94, 97.
49. Merrill, *First One Hundred Years*, p. 363; Goetzmann, *Army Exploration*, p. 397.
50. Goetzmann, *Exploration and Empire*, p. 316.

Chapter VI

THE PACIFIC RAILROAD SURVEYS

In 1853, with territorial expansion to the Pacific Ocean largely completed and railroads approaching the Mississippi River from the east, the time seemed ripe to consider building a transcontinental railway. A New York to Chicago line was completed in that year, and, in 1854, track reached the Father of Waters across the river from St. Louis. All the while, numerous railroad conventions—at Philadelphia in 1850, Iowa City in 1851, New Orleans in 1852—kept the matter before the people. Congress, urged by commercial interests and the general public to provide aid and encouragement for a Pacific railroad, began serious consideration of potential routes and forms of assistance.[1]

In the course of congressional consideration of three Pacific railway bills submitted during 1853, a limited consensus emerged. The legislators desired construction of a transcontinental line and agreed that substantial government aid was imperative. Rejecting as too costly the proposal of Illinois Senator Stephen A. Douglas for three routes, northern, central, and southern, the Senate concluded that only one line should be built. Here the general accord ended and the controversy began.[2]

The decision to support only one Pacific railroad precipitated a major sectional dispute. A Wisconsin newspaper stated the issue succinctly: "Shall the upper West or shall the lower West be the great avenue of trade and commerce?"[3] Because the upper West was free soil and the lower West was slave, the choice of a route and its terminals quickly became a national issue, pitting North against South. Thus divided, Congress failed to settle on any route across the continent.[4]

The dispute over the proposed line was also local and regional, with numerous western cities vying for the terminal. Promoters from St. Paul, Chicago, St. Louis, New Orleans, and other potential sites boosted their respective cities. Smaller towns, such as Fort Smith in Arkansas, also entered the lists. A German observer wryly noted: "Fort Smith, like every town in America, before it has well come into existence begins to think of establishing railroad connections...."[5]

Beset by so many contending interests, Congress finally abandoned the effort to settle on one best transcontinental route. Pennsylvania Senator Richard Brodhead's proposal for a reconnaissance of several potential lines by the Topographical Engineers, rejected early in the debate, was resurrected and passed as an amendment to the Army appropriation. The legislation took the difficult decision out of the hands of Congress and placed the burden on Secretary of War Jefferson Davis, who was charged with assigning survey teams to all prospective routes and selecting the best line based on the data compiled by field parties. Presumably, the topogs' impartial analysis would succeed where partisan politics failed.[6]

Bypassing the Topographical Bureau, Secretary Davis established a new agency, the Office of Pacific Railroad Explorations and Surveys, to administer the massive program. Under Major Emory until he departed in 1854 to survey the Gadsden Purchase line and then under Captain Andrew A. Humphreys, the office was charged with assessing the data generated by the surveys. This was a complex assignment: each expedition was required to report on the numerous determinants of railroad construction, among them distances, grades, mountain passes, canyons, bridgesites, and tunnels. In addition, each survey had to consider natural resources, particularly timber, stone, coal, and water, all of them important for building and operating a railroad. With a number of scientists, including geologists, minerologists, and naturalists accompanying each party and participating in the detailed inquiry, the surveys provided an outstanding opportunity for science to influence national policy.[7]

Of many possible transcontinental routes, four that had substantial congressional backing were chosen for scrutiny. The northernmost survey, led by former Engineer officer Isaac I. Stevens, examined a route between the forty-seventh and forty-ninth parallels from St. Paul, Minnesota, to Puget Sound. Captain John W. Gunnison led a party over a central route along the thirty-eighth parallel by way of the headwaters of the Arkansas to the Great Salt Lake. Further south, Lieutenant Amiel W. Whipple commanded the thirty-fifth parallel survey from Fort Smith to California via Albuquerque. The southernmost route along the thirty-second parallel, through Texas and the Gadsden Purchase, was surveyed by two expeditions, one under Lieutenant John Pope and another under Lieutenant John G. Parke. Other parties under Parke, and Lieutenants Henry L. Abbot and Robert S. Williamson probed the mountains of Oregon and California for railroad passes.

Hoping to deflect charges of bias toward his native South, Secretary of War Davis chose the survey leaders with great care. Davis had already come under fire for his appointment of Major Emory to head the administrative office. Senator Benton, who had strong commitments to the thirty-eighth parallel route, attacked the selection as proof of a predisposition toward Emory's own favorite route along the thirty-second parallel. Benton claimed that the red-whiskered Marylander, whose brother-in-law was president of a company planning a railway from Vicksburg to San Diego, owned shares in a San Diego real estate venture. As to the southernmost route itself, Benton thought the very idea absurd. Heaping ridicule on Emory, the topogs, and the Military Academy, he told his Senate colleagues that "it takes a grand national school like West Point to put national roads outside of a country and leave the interior without one."[8] With such opposition, Davis had to tread cautiously. Except for Lieutenant Pope, a native of slave-holding Kentucky, the leaders of the surveys were northerners all.[9]

Exploration began in the spring of 1853, when Stevens, the newly appointed governor of Washington Territory, led his expedition west from St. Paul. Able and energetic but biased toward the route that would serve Washington and the Pacific Northwest, Stevens controlled the largest and most elaborate of the surveys. The 240 men—11 officers, 76 enlisted men, and the rest scientists, teamsters, guides, and herders—faced the most difficult task of all the parties. Much of the vast region between St. Paul and Puget Sound had not been examined since Lewis and Clark crossed the continent in 1804-1806. Moreover, the susceptibility of the mountain passes to heavy snowfalls early in the autumn made speed essential. Stevens needed the large force assigned to him in order to complete the survey before winter.[10]

Stevens divided his men into several detachments, each with its own assignment. While he started westward across the plains, Captain George B. McClellan left Puget Sound to search for railroad passes through the mountains of the Pacific Northwest. Another party under Lieutenant Rufus Saxton established a depot at the western base of the Rockies and later surveyed a large portion of the region between the Columbia River valley and Fort Benton on the Missouri. Lieutenants Andrew Jackson Donelson and John Mullan went up the Missouri to create a supply base at Fort Union, a fur trading post far upstream, and examine the country.[11]

Still another small independent party under naturalist George Suckley spent a frigid month in the mountains. Sometimes eating roots to stay alive and huddling at night under eleven blankets and a buffalo robe to keep warm, Suckley accumulated a collection of natural history specimens nearly equal to that obtained by Stansbury's 1850 expedition to the Great Salt Lake. He and four companions built a canoe, packed the notebooks crammed with data on the courses of rivers and the specimens into the craft, and pushed off to rejoin their comrades at Fort Vancouver on the coast. They completed the remarkable journey of 1,049 miles in fifty-three days.[12]

Captain McClellan, assigned to investigate the passes through the Cascade Range, did not share Suckley's enthusiasm for winter in the Rockies. Characteristically cautious, McClellan halted operations when snow began to fall. "We must not," Stevens exhorted, "be frightened with long tunnels or enormous snows, but set ourselves to work to overcome them."[13] But no amount of urging could compel McClellan to brave the wintry mountains. Consequently, the survey never managed to determine the depths of snow in the Cascade passes.[14]

Skipping lightly over the problems presented by the mountains and severe north-country winters, Stevens called his route ideal. The extensive prairie, "easy character of the passes of the Rocky Mountains," good passes further west through the Couer d'Alenes and Cascades, and the

George B. McClellan. *National Archives.*

connection with oriental markets (Shanghai was only 5,000 miles from Puget Sound) made the northern line highly advantageous.[15] Some members of the expedition disagreed with the Governor of Washington regarding the desirability of the route through his Territory. Naturalist Suckley accused Stevens of outright puffery. The route was about as practicable as one through the Himalayas, he told his brother, adding that even most Washingtonians thought the most likely path was through South Pass.[16] For his uncle, Suckley had blunt advice: "If anybody should ask you to take stock in the road you had better decline...."[17] The truth lay somewhere between Steven's boosterism and Suckley's ridicule. The northern route would be possible but not easy.

The central route from St. Louis to the Pacific, strongly supported by St. Louis businessmen and Senator Benton, was examined by experienced and disinterested Captain John Gunnison. A veteran of eleven years service, Gunnison already had ample experience in the trans-Mississippi West, in the Indian Territory in 1841 and with Stansbury eight years later. Gunnison's assistant, artillery Lieutenant Edward G. Beckwith, was no tenderfoot. In 1849, after Captain Herman Thorn drowned in the Colorado, Beckwith had taken command of the detachment escorting the first collector of the Port of San Francisco across the Southwest.[18] Topographer Richard Kern and botanist Frederick Kreutzfeldt, both experienced frontiersmen, and geologist Jacob Schiel, a novice explorer, also accompanied Gunnison on his survey.

Gunnison's first few weeks in the field, from Westport Landing on the Missouri across the "graceful grassy swells of the Kansas prairie," resembled a pleasure trip. Two St. Louis sportsmen accompanied the expedition "for the recreation and sports of the chase." Not far behind, a small party of California-bound entrepreneurs drove their sheep and cattle along the trail blazed by the survey. Meanwhile, Gunnison amused himself and his men with efforts to obtain prairie dog specimens. He poured water into their holes and dug deep into the earth, but to no avail. Others in the party pursued the marmotlike rodents with rifles but also failed. The hunters from St. Louis, the herders, and the persistent efforts to capture the elusive prairie dogs all gave the expedition the atmosphere of a lark rather than a serious exploration.[19]

In August, 1853, as the party approached Sangre de Cristo Pass, the journey became increasingly difficult. Geologist Schiel, glad to leave the "eternal grass" of the plains as well as the mosquitoes, rattlesnakes, and other pests of the prairie, echoed innumerable travelers in his delight to see "the gigantic summits" of the Rockies. His pleasure was short-lived. Soon he joined the others, cursing and gasping for breath in the rarified atmosphere as they hacked their way over the timbered slopes of Sangre de Cristo in a daylong downpour. Finally, they put the crossing behind them and stopped for a well-earned rest at Fort Massachusetts in the San Juan valley.[20]

In need of a skilled guide for the rest of the journey, Gunnison left the party at Massachusetts and rode to Taos. Meanwhile, the men improved

John W. Gunnison. *National Archives.*

the road through the gap and fished the clear mountain streams for trout. In a few days Gunnison returned with experienced and well-known Antoine Leroux. A rarity among the mountainmen, this literate and wealthy New Mexico landowner and sheep rancher, scarred on scalp, arm, and wrist by arrow wounds, had already served as a member of the convention that organized New Mexico Territory. He still accepted jobs as guide, but his prosperity showed. Where Leroux went, his personal valet followed.[21]

Fort Massachusetts, Colorado, in 1855. *National Archives.*

The crucial question about the central route was whether a suitable pass existed between the San Juan valley and the plateau cut by the Grand and Green branches of the Colorado. Cochetopa Pass was known but unexplored. The approach to the pass was even more difficult than the climb up Sangre de Cristo. The party took four days to make the thirty miles to the top of the gap, bridging streams and hacking a wagon path through an aspen forest that extended to the crest. Geologist Schiel compared the task to "a continuous crossing of the Alps," without the comforts of mountain-climbing in such a populous region. He recalled some of the details of the arduous journey: "The wagons had to be dragged up steep mountains and be let down the steeper slopes with ropes;

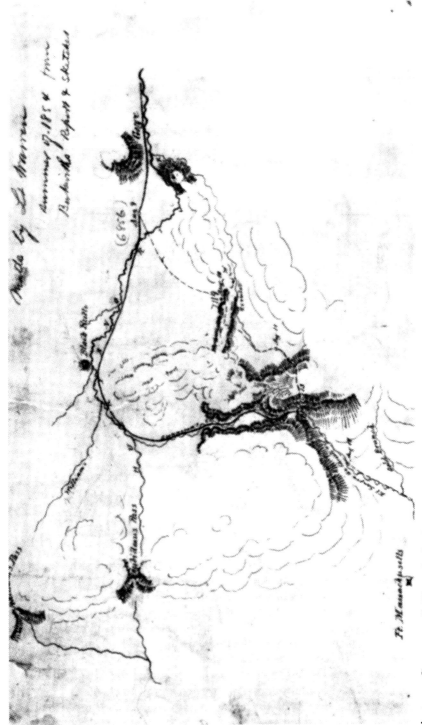

Lieutenant Gouverneur K. Warren's sketch of the Robideaux Pass vicinity, based on data acquired by the Gunnison expedition. *National Archives.*

rocky roads had to be cut through, ravines gone around, and strong mountain streams crossed...." Despite such obstacles, the party succeeded, and in the second week of September stood looking out over the valley of the Uncompahgre River (later renamed the Gunnison), the heart of Ute country.[22]

During the next four weeks Gunnison and his men crossed the divide between the Grand and Green rivers, then the Green itself. Green described the river, but not the valley. The plateau was barren and bone-dry, except for the soft shifting bed of the river that sped toward the Colorado. Lieutenant Beckwith saw problems for railroad construction: the porous sand would shift during the wet season and undermine the railbed.[23] Botanist Kreutzfeldt called the country alternately Sahara and Arabia and disliked it consistently. And he liked the sturdy, round-faced Ute warriors only a little more. Astounded and disgusted, he watched Gunnison establish what appeared to be a cordial understanding with the Indians, sometimes giving them gifts and other times trading for horses.[24] The Utes seemed peaceable enough and warned Gunnison that "across the mountains are bad Indians who kill white men...."[25]

While the expedition, with fresh horses and a Ute guide, struck westward toward the Great Basin, a sense of impending doom came over Kreutzfeldt. Well acquainted with mismanagement from his travels with Frémont during 1848-1849, Kreutzfeldt did not like what he saw. Several times Gunnison overrode Leroux's recommendations on campsites, only to spend the night at dry bivouacs. The captain, whom the botanist called "our uppermost scoundrel," "our ass of a captain," "the old dog," and worse, quarreled with Leroux the day before he left to fill a commitment to another expedition. Despite the argument, sparked when Gunnison ignored Leroux's advice to remain encamped while he reconnoitered the route ahead, the guide gave the topog directions to the Great Salt Lake. On September 24, Leroux departed. With Gunnison left to his own devices, Kreutzfeldt's anger became despair. Following a route he could not comprehend, "circles, curves, angles, and all kinds of figures, the theoreums of a Pythagoras could be enriched with," the botanist gave vent to extreme bitterness: "one is inclined to believe that this ass has lost his senses to lead us randomly through this unknown desert, which will probably lead us to misery...."[26]

On the night of October 24, Kreutzfeldt, shivering with cold, prepared to accompany Gunnison, Kern, guide William Potter, and eight others on an exploration of Sevier Lake. In the morning, the expedition split, Beckwith taking the main party northeastward while Gunnison camped along the Sevier River in a nook sheltered by the high bank and thick willows. A guard was posted over the bivouac, the men rested, and Kreutzfeldt contemplated "the captain's favorite project," the examination of "the damned Sevier Lake and river."[27]

As dawn broke on the 26th and the party breakfasted, a large band of Paiutes crept to within twenty-five yards of the small camp. Then, with a volley of rifle fire and a shower of arrows, they charged the sleepy encampment. Gunnison stepped from his tent and was cut down by a hail of arrows. Kern fell dead with a rifle ball in his heart. Six others, including Kreutzfeldt, also died in the surprise attack. Four men managed to get to their horses, flee the slaughter, and find Beckwith.[28]

Lieutenant Beckwith took command, regrouped his forces, and laid over for the winter in Salt Lake City. After backtracking to Fort Bridger in the spring, he finished the examination of the Great Basin along the forty-first parallel, and searched the Sierra Nevada for a suitable pass to California. His survey linked Captain Stansbury's discovery of a pass through the Rockies near Lodgepole Creek to Captain William Warner's California survey through Madeline Pass. The route he traced anticipated the path of the Union Pacific and Central Pacific railroads, the first transcontinental line actually built. His conclusion also verified the opinion Gunnison did not live to test, that the forty-first parallel offered a route more suitable than the thirty-eighth.[29]

Completion of the first Pacific railroad in 1869. *Library of Congress.*

To the south of the lines explored by Gunnison and Beckwith, Lieutenant Whipple led a party across the continent from Fort Smith to Los Angeles. Lieutenant Joseph C. Ives, less than a year out of West Point, accompanied him as assistant. Whipple had done his homework, studying the accounts of previous explorations by topogs Long, Abert, Simpson, and Sitgreaves. Moreover, like botanist John Bigelow, Whipple was a veteran of the boundary survey. Topographer Heinrich Möllhausen also came to the party with good credentials. He brought recommendations from the German scientist Alexander von Humboldt and Assistant Secretary Baird of the Smithsonian Institution. Möllhausen shared Whipple's enthusiasm and interest in the Indians, and praised the topog for his "special professional qualifications united [with] particularly pleasing manners which inspired confidence in all who approached him."[30]

The survey was perhaps the smoothest and most efficient of the several undertaken in 1853-1854. Whipple followed the Canadian River across the Indian Territory and the Texas panhandle, and left the river to cross the Pecos and Rio Grande near Albuquerque. The Rio Grande surprised Möllhausen, who expected a broad navigable stream with luxuriant vegetation but found "a shallow, muddy river [in] a treeless, clay-covered flat. . . ." Antoine Leroux, fresh from the Gunnison debacle, led Whipple over the San Francisco Mountains. Then two Mohaves showed the way through the Colorado basin into the Mohave Desert, which Whipple crossed to Cajon Pass through the Coast range.[31]

According to railroad engineer A. H. Campbell, who accompanied Whipple, only three points presented any difficulty. Even these, the crossings of the Pecos and Rio Grande and the route through Cajon Pass, were no more serious than the problems involved in building such trans-Allegheny lines as the Baltimore and Ohio from Cumberland, Maryland, to Wheeling, in western Virginia. Moreover, Whipple concluded that the thirty-fifth parallel route was particularly favored by precipitation. Both he and Campbell were well satisfied with the result of their exploration.[32]

The survey of the southwesternmost route along the thirty-second parallel also concluded satisfactorily. Two separate parties, both under topogs, examined this route. Lieutenant John Parke explored the western portion of the line, while Lieutenant John Pope, veteran of the 1849 reconnaissance of Minnesota and an 1851 survey of the Fort Leavenworth-Santa Fe road, probed the eastern section. His part of the survey included the greatest single obstacle, the *Llano Estacado* ("Staked Plains") that straddled the Texas-New Mexico border.

The Staked Plains severely tested those bold enough to attempt a crossing. Treeless and dry, the high, flat tableland stood a thousand feet or so above the rolling country to the east and west. Pope thought the region had excellent potential for cotton culture, and the tapping of underground sources of water in later years verified his evaluation. However, in early 1854, the Staked Plains was a formidable obstacle, and Pope's journal noted several nights spent at dry camps.[33]

Pope believed artesian wells would provide water for a railroad across the *Llano Estacado*. Alternate layers of hard and permeable rock, which trapped ground water, could be reached somewhere between 60 and 150 feet beneath the surface, and Pope recommended digging four wells to span the tableland. Four years later he was allowed to attempt drilling, but failed to develop reliable sources of water, due mainly to difficulties with his machinery. Geologist John Newberry still supported Pope, arguing that the experiment had good prospects for success. Events eventually proved them correct, but in the 1850's the Staked Plains refused to give up its water.[34]

To the west of Pope's section of the survey, Parke confronted similar

Lieutenant Whipple's Pacific railroad survey party camped in the Mohave Valley.

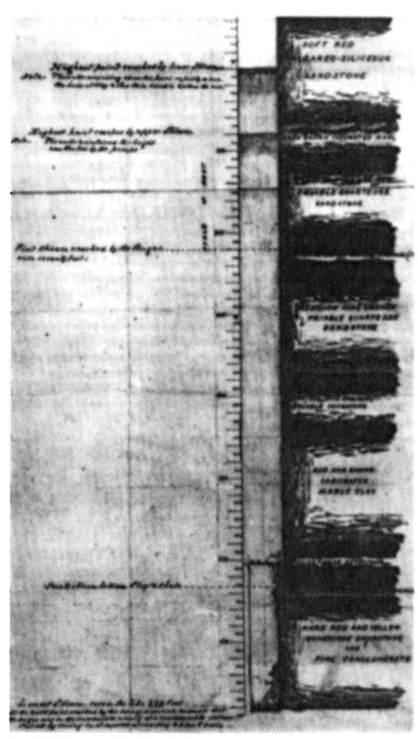

Lower half of a cross section of one of Lieutenant Pope's artesian wells. *National Archives.*

problems. He first visited the territory acquired in the Gadsden Purchase in early 1854, before ratification of the treaty by the Senate, and returned in the spring of the following year and improved his survey. Like Pope, he concluded that artesian wells would compensate for the lack of free-flowing water between the Gila and the Rio Grande.[35]

The four main route surveys, from the Parke-Pope explorations through the southwest to the Stevens expedition in the North, all probed east-west lines from the Mississippi River. In the far West a final pair of surveys ranged up and down the coast, examining mountain passes and possible connections between cities in California, Oregon, and Washington. These expeditions were conducted by three young topogs, Robert Williamson, John Parke, and Henry Abbot.

Williamson and Parke led one survey from San Francisco Bay down to San Diego. They examined the passes across the Sierra Madre eastward to the routes along the thirty-fifth and thirty-second parallels. Their expedition was far shorter than the cross-country treks but still difficult. Spending much of the time in the mountains, climbing steep slopes and crossing along narrow paths, they found that Cajon Pass and several others needed tunnels. More important, they did not find a practicable pass connecting San Diego to the Gila River along the thirty-second parallel. Williamson followed the Mohave River toward the Colorado, but gave up "with a mountainous country between and neither wood, water, nor grass that we know of." Meanwhile, Parke crossed the Coast range at Cajon Pass. All of the gaps except San Gorgonio, due east of Los Angeles, were too steep and required tunnels or roads cut along hillsides.[36]

Lieutenant Williamson's survey party at work near the entrance of Livermore Pass.

The other coastal expedition set out from Sacramento with two goals. Led first by Williamson and later Abbot after Williamson took ill, the party sought a suitable crossing of the Sierra Nevada near the source of the Carson River. In addition, their orders called for a survey of possible routes to Oregon and Washington. Because the Indians of northern California and Oregon were hostile, a large escort under Lieutenants John B. Hood, Philip Sheridan, Horatio Gates Gibson, and George Crook, accompanied the topogs. Williamson and Abbot were in good company as they started north to Klamath Lake.[37]

The surveyors also had some less-welcome companions. The country near Klamath was full of rattlesnakes. On the morning of 14 August 1855, "some excitement was created in camp by the discovery of a huge rattlesnake coiled up under a blanket." The men killed the reptile but remained uneasy for some time. As Abbot said, his men "all slept without tents on the ground, [and] unpleasant ideas were suggested by the incident."[38] Lest any of the party easily forget the rattler in the blanket, several more had to be killed at the evening's camp as well.

In spite of the snakes, the party continued northward for the examination of Oregon. Abbot's delight at "a magnificent lunar rainbow, and a beautifully tinted halo around the moon; both of which appeared at the same time in different quarters of the heavens," soon gave way to deep concern as news of Indian warfare reached him.[39] His Columbia River party numbered only seventeen, and a difficult and unknown country separated them from the settlements of the Willamette valley. Abbot made the dangerous ten-day trek with the help of an Indian guide, Sam An-ax-shal, whose skill saved him and his men from almost certain annihilation.

When he arrived at Oregon City near Fort Vancouver, Abbot received more bad news. Major Gabriel J. Rains, commander of the District of Puget Sound, had detained the entire escort at Fort Dalles for an operation against the Indians. Abbot's route lay through the Rogue River valley, the heart of the conflict, and his party had a mere five rifles. Letters of protest fell on deaf ears, and much of the survey had to be abandoned. Escorted through the Umpqua Canyon by a company of Oregon volunteers and later accompanied by Captain J. A. Smith's dragoons, Abbot managed to return to Fort Reading near Sacramento in mid-November. The last of the surveys had come to an end.

Captain Humphreys, assisted by Abbot and Lieutenant Gouverneur K. Warren, evaluated the data brought back by the field parties, and prepared cost estimates based on distances, terrain, and the experience of railroad builders east of the Mississippi. Calculations showed that all the proposed lines would be tremendously costly. Even the thirty-second parallel line, considered least expensive, would require $69 million, a sum equal to the entire federal budget of 1856. Then came the forty-first parallel route ($116 million) examined by Frémont and Stansbury in the previous decade as well as by Beckwith; Stevens's northern trail ($131 million); and finally Whipple's route ($169 million). No estimate was made for the thirty-eighth parallel route, generally conceded to be impracticable.[40]

Although the cost estimates indicated that the southernmost route was least expensive, the results were inconclusive for two reasons. In the first place, Lieutenant Williamson's inability to locate a pass between San Diego and the Gila River cast some doubt over the suitability of that line. More important in light of the political character of the problem of route selection, the surveys revealed that the three more costly paths were nevertheless practicable. Indeed, after the Civil War transcontinental lines were built on or near all four routes. For the time, the congressional deadlock persisted, and the surveys, designed to clarify the issue, only clouded it.[41]

As a scientific enterprise, on the other hand, the Pacific railroad project had remarkable and enduring results. The naturalists, collectors, and artists who accompanied the field parties amassed a vast quantity of specimens and scientific data. With the help of scholars in eastern cities, this accumulation was assessed and organized into a comprehensive record of the trans-Mississippi region's fauna and flora, geological structure, and geographical features. The thirteen-volume final report, along with four preliminary volumes, became immediately famous. The huge compendium was widely discussed in the daily press, popular magazines, and in the streets and homes of America.[42] The report is still well known to naturalists. As A. Hunter Dupree concluded in his study of the federal government and science, "to the student of the fauna, flora, and geology of the West, the volumes still seem as live and as important as they seem futile to the political historian."[43]

An important result of the railroad surveys was Lieutenant Warren's map of the trans-Mississippi West. Interrupted twice so that he could complete western explorations of his own, Warren toiled long hours when he was in his Washington office. Lieutenant Abbot, who worked with Warren in the Office of Pacific Railroad Surveys and Explorations, later recalled "how the midnight hour often found him hard at work comparing and reconstructing his preliminary tracings, or poring over the old reports for missing data."[44] The completion of this cartographic milestone marked the close of an era for the Engineers. The white spaces on Warren's map still remained to be filled and new questions would arise and demand answers, but an essential task was now complete. For nearly forty years, since Long's expedition of 1819-1820, Engineer parties had charted portions of the vast West. Some of the maps, most notably those done by Preuss after his travels with Frémont, were themselves highly significant. But they were also part of the overall effort to understand and record the shape of the new country. In 1858, the basic contours of the enormous region were at last known and the information readily available.[45]

Notes

1. Robert E. Riegel, *The Story of the Western Railroads* (New York: Macmillan, 1926), pp. 4, 6, 19; Robert T. Russel, *Improvement of Communication with the Pacific Coast as an Issue in American Politics 1783-1864* (Cedar Rapids: Torch Press, 1948), p. 95.
2. Russel, *Improvement of Communication*, pp. 96-99; Allan Nevins, *Ordeal of the Union*, II (New York: Charles Scribner's Sons, 1947), p. 87; Carter Goodrich, *Government Promotion of American Canals and Railroads 1800-1890* (New York: Columbia University Press, 1960), pp. 179, 182.
3. Grant County (Wisconsin) *Herald*, quoted in Goodrich, *Government Promotion*, p. 179.
4. Riegel, *Western Railroads*, p. 15; Goodrich, *Government Promotion*, p. 179.
5. Heinrich B. Möllhausen, *Diary of a Journey from the Mississippi to the Coast of the Pacific*, ed. by Peter A. Fritzell, I (New York: Johnson Reprint Corp., 1969), p. 11.
6. Russel, *Improvement of Communication*, pp. 100, 107-08; Goetzmann, *Army Exploration*, p. 262; 10 *Stat.* 219 (3 March 1853).
7. Russel, *Improvement of Communication*, p. 174; Goetzmann, *Army Exploration*, pp. 274-75; Ryan, "War Department Topographical Bureau," p. 185.
8. Goetzmann, *Army Exploration*, p. 267.
9. Russel, *Improvement of Communication*, p. 168.
10. Hazard Stevens, *The Life of Isaac Ingalls Stevens*, I (Boston: Houghton, Mifflin, 1900), p. 307; Goetzmann, *Army Exploration*, p. 281; Oscar O. Winther, "Early Commercial Importance of the Mullan Road," *Oregon Historical Quarterly*, 46 (March 1945), 22.
11. Isaac I. Stevens, *Report of Exploration of a Route for the Pacific Railroad, Near the Forty-Seventh and Forty-Ninth Parallels, from St. Paul to Puget Sound*, 33d Cong., 1st sess., House of Representatives Executive Document 129, I, pp. 4-5.
12. George Suckley to Rutsen Suckley, 9 December 1853, Suckley Papers, Yale University.
13. Quoted in Hazard Stevens, *Isaac Ingalls Stevens*, I, p. 290.
14. Hazard Stevens, *Isaac Ingalls Stevens*, I, pp. 290-91.
15. Isaac Stevens, *Report*, pp. 11, 49-50.
16. Suckley to John Suckley, 25 January 1854, Suckley Papers.
17. Suckley to Rutsen Suckley, 9 December 1853, Suckley Papers.
18. Edwards, ed., *The Whipple Report*, pp. 61-62.
19. Edward G. Beckwith, *Report of Exploration of a Route for the Pacific Railroad, near the 38th and 39th Parallels of Latitude, From the Mouth of the Kansas to Sevier River, in the Great Basin*, 33d Cong.,

1st sess., House of Representatives Executive Document 129, II, pp. 4-6, 22, 24.

20. Jacob H. Schiel, *Journey Through the Rocky Mountains and the Humboldt Mountains to the Pacific Ocean*, ed. by Thomas N. Bonner (Norman: University of Oklahoma Press, 1959), pp. 25, 29; Beckwith, *Exploration near the 38th and 39th Parallels*, p. 35; Frederick Kreutzfeldt, "Memorandum Book of Mr. Kreutzfeldt," trans. by Sylvia Envers, Kreutzfeldt Papers, Smithsonian Institution.

21. Beckwith, *Exploration near the 38th and 39th Parallels*, pp. 35-36, 39-43; Kreutzfeldt, "Memorandum Book"; Forbes Parkhill, "Antoine Leroux," in *The Mountain Men and the Fur Trade of the Far West*, ed. by Leroy R. Hafen, IV (Glendale, Calif.: Arthur H. Clark, 1966), pp. 177-83.

22. Schiel, *Journey Through the Rocky Mountains*, pp. 43-45.

23. Beckwith, *Exploration near the 38th and 39th Parallels*, pp. 56-73.

24. Kreutzfeldt, "Memorandum Book."

25. Schiel, *Journey Through the Rocky Mountains*, p. 54.

26. Kreutzfeldt, "Memorandum Book."

27. Kreutzfeldt, "Memorandum Book"; Beckwith, *Exploration near the 38th and 39th Parallels*, pp. 79-82.

28. Beckwith, *Exploration near the 38th and 39th Parallels*, pp. 81-83; Hine, *Edward Kern*, pp. 96-97; Schiel, *Journey Through the Rocky Mountains*, p. 67.

29. Beckwith, *Report of Explorations for the Pacific Railroad On the Line of the Forty-first Parallel of North Latitude*, 33d Cong., 1st sess., House of Representatives Executive Document 129, II, pp. 5, 13-15, 18, 41, 72; Goetzmann, *Army Exploration*, pp. 285-86; Goetzmann, *Exploration and Empire*, p. 388.

30. Amiel W. Whipple, *Report of Exploration for a Railway Route, Near the Thirty-fifth Parallel of Latitude, from the Mississippi River to the Pacific Ocean*, 33d Cong., 1st sess., House of Representatives Executive Document 129, II, p. 7, 10, 21; Möllhausen, *Diary*, I, p. 15; Spencer F. Baird to Scientific Men throughout North America, 31 May 1853, Baird Papers, Smithsonian Institution.

31. Whipple, *Report*, pp. 23, 27, 32; Möllhausen, *Diary*, I, p. 331; Robert Taft, *Artists and Illustrators of the Old West, 1850-1900* (New York: Bonanza Books, n. d.), pp. 26-27.

32. Whipple, *Report*, pp. 34-40, 82-83, 86.

33. W. Eugene Hollon, *The Southwest: Old and New* (Lincoln: University of Nebraska Press, 1968), p. 15; W. Eugene Hollon, *Beyond the Cross Timbers, The Travels of Randolph B. Marcy, 1812-1887* (Norman: University of Oklahoma Press,1955), pp. 69-70; Martin Crimmins, "Captain John Pope's Route to the Pacific," *The Military Engineer*, 23 (March–April 1931), 158; John Pope, *Report of Exploration of a Route for the Pacific Railroad, Near the Thirty-second Parallel of Latitude, From the Red River to the Rio Grande*, 33d Cong., 1st sess., House of Representatives Executive Document

129, II, pp. 72, 92, 94-95.

34. Pope, *Report*, pp. 15, 48-49; Goetzmann, *Exploration and Empire*, p. 274; Newberry, "Geological Report," p. 51.

35. John G. Parke, *Report of Explorations for Railroad Routes from San Francisco Bay to Los Angeles, California, West of the Coast Range, and from the Pimas Villages on the Gila to the Rio Grande, Near the 32d Parallel of North Latitude*, 33d Cong., 2d sess., Senate Executive Document 78, VII, pp. 3, 20; Goetzmann, *Army Exploration*, p. 290; Wallace, *The Great Reconnaissance*, p. 198.

36. Robert S. Williamson, *Report Upon the Routes in California to Connect with the Routes near the Thirty-fifth and Thirty-second Parallels*, 33d Cong., 2d sess., Senate Executive Document 78, V, pp. 7, 9, 27, 30-32, 34-36, 39; Goetzmann, *Army Exploration*, pp. 292-93.

37. Henry L. Abbot, *Report of Lieut. Henry L. Abbot, Corps of Topographical Engineers, Upon Explorations for a Railroad Route, from the Sacramento Valley to the Columbia River*, 33d Cong., 2d sess., Senate Executive Document 78, VI, pp. 9-10, 59, 62. The following account of the Abbot expedition is based on this report. Footnotes are provided only for portions quoted in the text.

38. Abbot, *From the Sacramento Valley to the Columbia*, p. 66.

39. Abbot, *From the Sacramento Valley to the Columbia*, p. 90.

40. Goodrich, *Government Promotion*, p. 332; *The Statistical History of the United States from Colonial Times to the Present* (Stamford, Conn.: Fairfield Publishers, 1965), p. 711. Whipple's estimate was later found to be excessive and was halved. Goetzmann, *Army Exploration*, p. 312.

41. Goetzmann, *Army Exploration*, pp. 295, 298, 300, 303-04; Goetzmann, *Exploration and Empire*, p. 292; Oscar O. Winther, *The Transportation Frontier, Trans-Mississippi West, 1865-1890* (New York: Holt, Rinehart, and Winston, 1964), p. 99.

42. Goetzmann, *Army Exploration*, pp. 307, 312, 336; Taft, *Artists and Illustrators*, p. 5; George P. Merrill, *First One Hundred Years of American Geology*, pp. 310-11.

43. Dupree, *Science in the Federal Government*, p. 95.

44. Henry L. Abbot, "Memoir of Gouverneur Kemble Warren,1830-1832," Warren Papers, New York State Library, Albany.

45. Goetzmann, *Army Exploration*, p. 313; Gilbert, *The Exploration of Western America*, pp. 202-03; Wheat, "Mapping the American West, 1540-1857," pp. 164-65.

Chapter VII

FILLING IN THE BLANKS:
THE NORTHERN FRONTIER, 1855-1860

When Lieutenant Warren reported for duty with the Office of Pacific Railroad Explorations and Surveys in 1854, he already carried a reputation for uncommon intelligence and ability. Only a year after he had graduated second in the West Point class of 1850, rumors circulated regarding his return to the Academy as a mathematics instructor. But the strikingly handsome black-haired and moustached officer longed for adventure instead of the classroom. "I would rather rough it," he told his father, "than be sent there before hard service had made me above reproach."[1] He spent the next three years on the western rivers, first on the Mississippi Delta survey under Captain Humphreys, then on the board for improvement of the Louisville and Portland Canal on the Ohio, and finally on an examination of the Rock Island and Des Moines rapids.[2] The poise and self-assurance gained during this apprenticeship showed in his letters to his Cold Springs, New York, home. His early missives had been signed "Gouverneur K. Warren, U.S.A.," but later correspondence was inscribed by a more confident "Gouv." Warren was ready for his important assignment of compiling the map of the trans-Mississippi West.

As Warren assembled the data for his map, the blank spaces in knowledge of the West became apparent. In addition to the Yellowstone and Colorado wonderlands, much of the vast new Nebraska Territory, which included the modern states of Nebraska, North Dakota, South Dakota, and parts of Wyoming and Montana, was largely unexplored. Nicollet had examined much of the region north of the Missouri River, and untold numbers of travelers had crossed along the Platte. Only traders and trappers knew much about the region between the rivers, the Nebraska sandhills, the Black Hills homeland of the Sioux, and the tributaries Loup, Niobrara, and Yellowstone. These major gaps in geographical knowledge, if left unfilled, would mean large white spaces on the map.

Far from Warren's Capitol Hill office, on the North Platte near Fort Laramie, other events underscored the need for information on Nebraska Territory. In August, 1854, after a Miniconjou Sioux warrior living with a Brulé band stole a Mormon emigrant's cow, Lieutenant John L. Grattan and a detachment of soldiers entered the Indian camp, set up artillery, and demanded the surrender of the culprit. When the Brulé chief Conquering

Gouverneur K. Warren as a West Point cadet. *U.S. Military Academy Archives.*

Bear stalled, Grattan opened fire. Conquering Bear fell in the first volley. Then the Sioux attacked the soldiers, killing Grattan and thirty-one of his men. Only one trooper managed to flee to Fort Laramie. Thus did 1854 become known among the Sioux as *Mato wayuhi ktepi* ("the year in which Conquering Bear was killed").[3]

The whites called the affair the Grattan Massacre and sent an expedition under Colonel William S. Harney to punish the Indians for the incident and for their raids on Platte River emigrant parties. Because little was known about the Sioux hunting grounds on the northern plains, Harney needed the services of a topographical Engineer. The initial choice was Captain Thomas J. Lee, but he resigned to avoid the disagreeable duty of chastising Indians. The task then fell to Lieutenant Warren. In the summer of 1855, with his map scarcely begun, he left Washington. Inaugurating a period of Army exploration on the high plains, Warren would get the opportunity to fill some of the spaces on his map.[4]

Warren prepared for his assignment in St. Louis. He studied the maps of Frémont and Stansbury and talked to frontier-wise traders about the Sioux. He also folded into his journal a copy of "Instructions for Astronomical & Magnetic Party," which Lieutenant Whipple had originally prepared for use by Lieutenant Ives. Warren also penned reminders to himself on the care of his equipment: "All instruments should be handled lightly and delicately. No clamp screws should be tightly pressed. Every part of an instrument not absolutely necessary should be dispensed with. . . ."[5] On 7 June 1855, well primed for his first frontier assignment, he boarded a Missouri River steamer bound for Fort Pierre.[6]

Warren started upriver before Harney and the main force left St. Louis. The two officers planned to meet later in the summer at Fort Kearny on the North Platte. Meanwhile, Warren would mark off and survey a military reservation for Fort Pierre, just purchased from the American Fur Company, in preparation for Harney's campaign. On his way upriver, Warren started a sketch map but, discovering that his drawings agreed with Nicollet's map, gave up the endeavor. Once at Fort Pierre, he surveyed the military reservation under a July sun that burned so bright the soldier who carried his theodolite collapsed with sunstroke. With the work completed in early August, Warren made ready to join Harney on the Platte.[7]

Because the 300-mile stretch between Fort Pierre and the Fort Kearny rendezvous was barely known and unmapped, Warren planned carefully before setting out on the trek. He closely questioned the beavermen at Pierre regarding the terrain, purchased animals, and hired six of the trappers as guides and escort. Then he slipped quietly out of the fort with his party, south across the White River, which was Smoky Earth to the Sioux. Then came a stream of many names: Niobrara the Anglo-Americans called it, but the French voyageurs said *L'eau qui Court* and the Sioux Running Water. South of the river, which raced east to the Missouri, were the sandhills, "exceedingly solitary, silent and desolate and depressing," Warren said.[8] The mules sank to their forelocks as they plodded through the dune country, which the Sioux and their Pawnee enemies crossed when they raided each other's villages for horses. Fortunately, the party met neither tribe. After two weeks spent making a topographical sketch and noting the locations of the travelers' essentials—wood, water, and grass—Warren sighted Fort Kearny, where the trails from the jumping off places on the Missouri merged into the main trunkline of the Platte River road. Warren's appearance delighted

Harney, who served champagne to celebrate the young officer's safe arrival.[9]

Established in 1849 by Engineer Lieutenant Daniel P. Woodbury to protect travelers on the Oregon Trail, Fort Kearny served as the staging area for Harney's swift and overpowering thrust at the Brulé tribe. In late August, 1855, with Warren and his small corps of guides and interpreters, Harney assembled his expedition. About 600 soldiers, infantry, cavalry, and artillery, stirred up a huge dustcloud as they left the fort to avenge the death of Lieutenant Grattan and halt the Indian raids along the Platte.[10]

In just a few days, Harney located his foe and got his fight. On September 2, while camped near Ash Hollow on the North Platte, Warren sighted Little Thunder's camp. Wasting no time, Harney deployed his forces for an attack on the following morning. When the Indians began to flee at the sight of the troops, Harney lured them back with a request for a parley. The ploy worked, and the soldiers struck. The Brulés tried to escape their overwhelming enemy, but Harney pursued them relentlessly. While Warren watched from a hilltop, the troops scattered the Sioux and killed more than eighty of them.[11]

Although the thorough rout ended the day's labor for most of the soldiers, Warren's work had just begun. He tried to make a topographical sketch of the scene, but soon turned his attention instead to the wounded women and children, crying and moaning all around him. After carrying to safety a little Indian girl who had been injured in the battle, he joined others in a search for more of the wounded. He found another young girl, shot through both feet, and a boy with multiple leg wounds. Another soldier helped him carry the children to a stream, where they made a shelter to protect them from the sun and bathed their wounds. While Warren aided the survivors, others boasted of their heroism in the one-sided fight. "I was," Warren wrote, "disgusted with the tales of valor in the field, for there were but few who killed anything but a flying foe."[12] Untroubled by such thoughts, the soldiers sang as they left Ash Hollow:

We did not make a blunder,
We rubbed out Little Thunder
And we sent him to the other side of Jordan.[13]

At the end of the summer, after accompanying Harney to Fort Laramie and into the Sioux hunting grounds north of the Platte, Warren turned to his report and map. Back at the office in Washington, he organized his notes on the journey and prepared a map of his route. With meteorologist J. Hudson Snowden, Warren spent long hours arranging his data on the weather. In mid-March, 1856, he finished his report on his travels. While draftsmen Edwin Freyhold and F. W. Egloffstein added his findings to the general map of the trans-Mississippi West, he turned to organizing a party for a second trip to the northern plains. Before the end of April, Warren was again in St. Louis, waiting for a riverboat with Snowden, topographer W. H. Hutton, and geologist Ferdinand V. Hayden.[14]

Although the journey to Fort Pierre began on the steamer *Genoa*, it ended as a long hike. Warren enjoyed riverboat travel but grew impatient

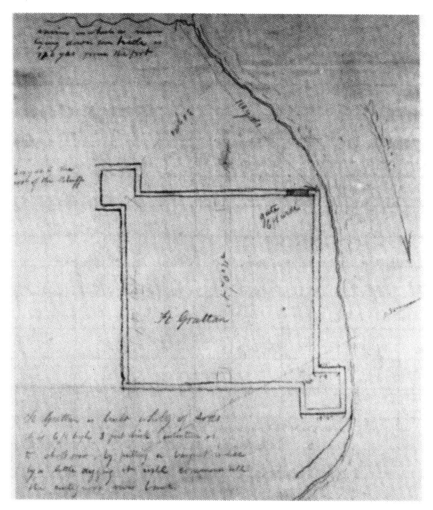

After the fight at Ash Hollow, Warren drew this plan for a sod fort, which was built by Harney's men and named Fort Grattan. *New York State Library.*

as the *Genoa* struggled against wind and current. Finally, when the vessel ran aground on a sandbar in the shallows near the mouth of Running Water, he, the Fort Pierre sutler, and three others set out overland for the post. They walked 160 miles, subsisting mainly on birds brought down with shotguns. Although the journey was hard, Warren welcomed the chance to examine the terrain away from the river. On 21 May 1856, the lieutenant reported to Colonel Harney at Fort Pierre. He and his companions had beaten the *Genoa* by three days.[15]

Upon his arrival, Warren found the colonel in council with most of the important Sioux chiefs. Harney, whose show of force in the previous year had put a stop to the raids, introduced Warren to the assembled headmen and told them the topog would spend the summer reconnoitering the

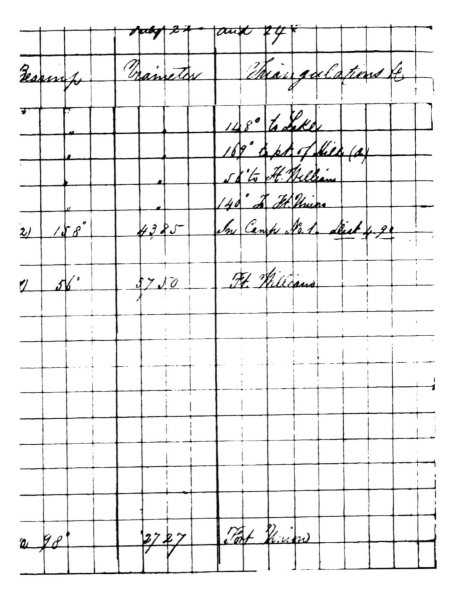

These pages from William Hutton's 1856 journal show his notes and his drawing of the Missouri River near the mouth of the Yellowstone. *New York State Library.*

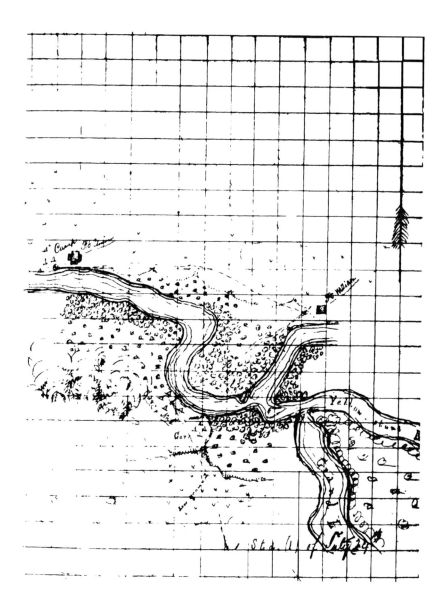

upper Missouri. Mindful of the devastating blow dealt Little Thunder, the chiefs agreed to allow Warren to go unmolested.[16]

Reunited with the members of his party who arrived on the *Genoa*, Warren boarded the American Fur Company steamer *St. Mary* for the rest of the journey up the Missouri. Reinforced by seventeen men of Harney's Second Infantry and equipped with the usual scientific instruments— astronomical transit, sextant, chronometers, barometers, odometers, and compasses—he went far up river, past the fur-trading post at Fort Union into present-day Montana. Hutton sketched the Missouri almost as far as the site of modern Fort Peck dam, then turned back to Fort Union. Jim Bridger joined the expedition and led the way down uncharted portions of the Yellowstone to the mouth of the Powder. Warren kept an eye out for potential fort sites while gathering data for his map.[17] Living off the land was easy. He and his men "enjoyed the greatest abundance of large game of all kinds while on the Yellowstone. . . ."[18] With the completion of his reconnaissance of this river, another blank space was filled.

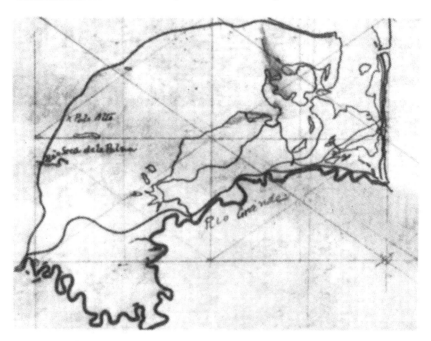

Warren's reduction of Lieutenant Joseph Webster's map of the mouth of the Rio Grande. *National Archives.*

Accompanied by his assistants and escort, Warren began the month-long trip back to Fort Pierre on the first of September. Most of the party paddled down the Missouri in a bullboat, a flat-bottomed craft made of Buffalo skins stretched over a cottonwood frame, while a shore party of seven herded the animals. Warren stopped at the mouths of tributaries to take readings on their positions and examine the country. His progress was uneventful until the eighteen-foot-long boat struck a sandbar near

Fort Pierre and spun broadside against the current. The men quickly leaped into the 40° water and freed the craft before it became uncontrollable. With an eye on the Indians who watched from shore, Hutton noted that the party "presented an appearance much more interesting to our enemies than agreeable to our friends."[19] Warren reached Pierre safely, released his escort, and continued downriver to Sioux City. From there travel became easier and more comfortable, as he took a steamboat to St. Louis and finished the journey to Washington by rail.[20]

Back at his desk, Warren returned to the complex task of assembling data for the great map. In the topographical memoir that accompanied the map, he explained his method: "The plan . . . has been to represent only such portions as have been actually explored, and of which our information may be considered reliable."[21] To accomplish this, Warren had to be as much historian as cartographer. He studied the maps and records of the Pacific Railroad Surveys, the United States Land Office, Coast Survey, and Mexican Boundary Commission, as well as the large map file in the Topographical Bureau. The Indian Bureau and the Smithsonian Institution also contributed books and maps. From all of this overlapping and sometimes conflicting material, he had to select the best data.

Although Warren's standards were sensible, his choice of authorities proved a major problem. When maps showed different locations for a town or topographical feature, he used "the work of those explorers who were best provided with instruments, and who possessed the largest share of that experience which is so necessary in attaining accuracy, taking the evidence of these advantages from their own reports."[22] Sometimes, when he was unable to choose from the results of several able explorers, he opted for an average reading. In the case of Fort Smith, for example, Warren had to take an average of five longitudinal readings made by able and reliable explorers from Long in 1820 to Whipple in 1853.[23] Thus the map lacked real precision, although the deviations between findings of conflicting authorities were usually trivial.

Nevertheless, blatant inaccuracies and guesses were absent. The history of western cartography was filled with myth, rumor, and fantasy, but Warren stuck to reliable data. Where the facts were unknown, the map sheet was left blank: "In some large sections," he explained, "we possess no information, except from uncertain sources. In these parts the rule was adopted to leave the map blank, or to faintly indicate such information as is probably correct."[24]

With all the determinations made, Warren turned the map over to draftsmen Freyhold and Egloffstein, and once again returned to Nebraska. This probe, up the Loup to the sandhills and then along the Niobrara to Fort Laramie and back through the Black Hills, proved to be the most difficult and dangerous of his three northern plains expeditions. His troubles included Loup River quicksand, the ubiquitous Platte valley mosquitoes, the Sioux, and even his military escort. Before he set out for the mouth of the Loup, most of his twenty-seven-man escort became drunk and insubordinate. Twelve of the soldiers, "tempted," Warren said, "by the high price of labor in this vicinity, and tired of the toils and privations of campaigning," deserted, and thieves stole two of the party's horses. Still near Sioux City, Warren wondered what might befall him in less hospitable surroundings: "These losses occuring in a civilized community, where we supposed ourselves among friends, were quite annoying, and gave rather unpleasant forebodings of what might occur to us when we should come among our enemies, the Indians."[25]

Quicksand, rain, and plain hard work marked the journey into the sandhills. The bed of the North Loup was so treacherous that a wagon sank clear to its bed as the party tried to cross the river. The men had to wade into the muck and haul the baggage ashore, then extricate the vehicle. Later, they bridged several streams on their way northwest. One man became seriously ill and had to ride in a wagon, which was fine until a jackrabbit stampeded the herd and sent the ambulance careening down a steep hill. Fortunately the conveyance remained upright, and the party finished the journey to the head of the Loup safely.[26] The reconnaissance filled a small white space on the map, but Warren wondered if the effort was worthwhile:

> We have now traced the river from end to end and found its impracticability for almost any purpose so marked that it seems like a great waste of time to have made the exertions we have. Our greatest wish is to get away from it as soon as possible and never return.[27]

The trip up the Loup had been hard but at least there had been water. For their first two days in the dune country, the party failed to find a drop of the precious fluid. On August 9, Warren sighted a lake in the distance, and the men rushed forward, only to find it "so salt and bitter that a mule would not drink it."[28] They managed to get some palatable water by digging a hole in the sand. Two days later a driving rain came to their rescue. They collected the water in barrels for the remainder of the trek to the Niobrara, which was only a short distance away but difficult to reach because the sandhills forced them to take a southwesterly course away from the river. They took more than a week to cross the short distance between the head of the Loup and Running Water.

The bone-weary travelers found the remainder of the journey to Fort Laramie much easier. The striking wind-cut formations of the upper reaches of Running Water, which reminded Snowden of ruins of ancient forts and castles, did not impede their progress. On August 18, they looked down on the valley of the North Platte, and "the prospect of reaching Laramie cheered everyone."[29] On the next day, Warren's exhausted party arrived at the post for a well-earned rest.

Warren laid over at Fort Laramie for two weeks, planning a reconnaissance into the Black Hills. The hills were sacred to the Sioux, who called the region *Pa Sapa* ("Black Heads"), for in the distance the dense pines indeed looked black, but Warren had reason to believe that

124

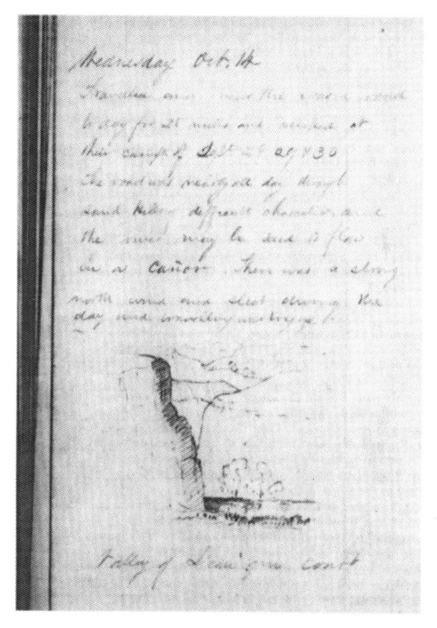

A page from Warren's 1857 journal, showing the canyon of the Niobrara. *New York State Library.*

they would let him pass in peace. When he had met Little Thunder's band on the way up Running Water, they had fled in terror. Moreover, Major Thomas Twiss, the Indian agent at Fort Laramie, also thought the Sioux would not trouble Warren. They had complained to Twiss, but appeared satisfied with assurance that Warren would not make a road through *Pa Sapa*.[30]

While Warren outfitted a packtrain for the expedition, P. M. Engel of his party scaled Laramie Peak. The massive mountain, about thirty miles west of the fort, towered 6,000 feet above the surrounding plateau. Engel climbed past the timberline to the rocky crest, from which he looked south on the beautiful valley of the Laramie River. "The most splendid grass" covered the Laramie plain, one day to become excellent grazing country.[31]

Engel's safe passage may have helped assure Warren of an unmolested journey through the Black Hills. The day before he set out, he wrote his father that the great display of force then in progress "completely overawed" the Indians. And, indeed, the North Platte was the scene of a great deal of military activity. Troops bound for Utah, where war with the Mormons was imminent, passed Fort Laramie, as did a column operating against the Cheyennes. In addition to these and Warren's own party, a fellow topog, Lieutenant Francis T. Bryan, was in the field exploring a potential railroad route south of Fort Laramie, up Lodgepole Creek to Bridger Pass. Supposing that all this activity impressed and puzzled the Sioux, Warren set out for the Black Hills, expecting a hard but fruitful journey.[32]

Snowden and a portion of the expedition remained at Laramie preparing to examine the Niobrara before meeting Warren downstream, east of the hills in mid-October. Those who stayed got more than enough trader whiskey, a rank mixture sometimes spiked with chewing tobacco, red peppers, and even rattlesnake heads, and discipline began to weaken. Ten days, one desertion, and two horsethefts after Warren left, Snowden led his party toward the source of Running Water, east of the modern Nebraska-Wyoming line near the yet undiscovered deposits of dinosaur bones at Agate Springs. Once cheered by the sight of Laramie's adobe walls, Snowden now was happy to put the post behind him.[33]

Contrary to Warren's expectations, the Sioux blocked his path through the Black Hills. Shortly after his entrance near the peak known as *Inyan Kara* to the Sioux, a large force of warriors under the Huncpapa Bear's Rib demanded that Warren turn back. Bear's Rib was very persuasive. He feared that Warren would spook the buffalo, but dreaded even more the potential military value of the reconnaissance. The angry warriors with him were even more convincing. Bear's Rib granted permission for Warren to leave by a northern route, and the lieutenant wisely accepted. He cut across what is now the Pine Ridge Indian Reservation, camping on Wounded Knee Creek before following the Keya Paha to its junction with Running Water. He found Snowden on October 15, making his way downstream along the northern fringe of the sandhills.[34]

Snowden, who endured "a very tortuous and fatiguing march, as bad if not worse than any of our sandhills experience," also confronted an angry Sioux party.[35] On October 11, Brulé warriors stopped him and complained that Harney had assured them no whites would pass through their lands without a license from him (they did not know—and probably would not have cared if they did—that Congress had repudiated Harney's agreements). The Indians protested Snowden's profligate consumption of the resources along Running Water, the plums and chokecherries, wood and grass. Moreover, they angrily accused the whites of frightening the wild game for a hundred miles in every direction. Snowden had to threaten to open fire before the Sioux finally withdrew from his camp.[36]

Reunited on October 15, Warren and Snowden traveled to Fort Randall while Engel followed the Niobrara to its confluence with the Missouri. The trip from Laramie had been hazardous for both divisions, but Warren had obtained important information about the river. His reconnaissance convinced him of the impossibility of road construction in the Niobrara valley. The upper two-thirds of the stream ran swift and shallow through deep-cut canyons. The lower portion, wider than the Missouri, was almost impossible to cross due to the treacherous bottom. Warren discouraged consideration of a proposed road from Lake Superior southwestward across Minnesota, Dakota, and Nebraska to the Platte and South Pass. Such a trail would have to cross Running Water three times. Besides, the Sioux would oppose such an effort. Anyone bold enough to attempt a road survey through their hunting grounds would need at least two hundred tried men. Warren was convinced "the Sioux are in earnest about stopping white men from coming there anymore."[37]

Carefully Lieutenant Warren pondered the difficulties confronting the Sioux and their options. He had developed great respect for the seven tribes—the Oglala, Brulé, Huncpapa, Sans Arc, Miniconjou, Blackfoot, and Two Kettle—of the Teton Sioux. Like most whites he erred in calling the seven autonomous tribes, each in turn divided into seven bands, a nation. But he made no mistake about their military skill and determination to defend their homeland. They were superb horsemen, "numerous, independent, warlike, and powerful. . . ." and had the strength and will for "prolonged and able resistance to further encroachment of the western settlers."[38]

While he knew that efforts to dislodge the Sioux would bring war, he also recognized that the attempt would nonetheless be made. The incessant pressure of white pioneers, combined with the process of Indian dispossession to the east of the Sioux domains, hastened war. Indians evicted from their land and forced west ultimately exerted pressure on the resources available to plains natives. This, in turn, caused poverty and disease, while the government exacerbated these ills by its failure to protect and support the dispossessed. Concluding this sophisticated analysis, Warren said there were "so many inevitable causes at work to produce a war with the Dakotas before many years, that I regard the greatest fruit of the explorations I have conducted to be the knowledge of the proper routes by which to invade their country and conquer them."[39] He was not particularly proud of this accomplishment: "I almost feel guilty of crime in being a pioneer to the white men who will ere long drive the red man from his last niche of hunting ground."[40]

Warren also laid bare the dilemma that faced Sioux leaders who understood the inevitable result of the process then underway. Bear's Rib, for example, a man with "fine mental powers and proper appreciation of the relative power of his people and the whites . . .'' trod a very narrow and dangerous path, knowing that surrender would make him an outcast but that advocacy of resistance would make him responsible for the destruction of the tribe.[41] Ultimately the Huncpapa chief's personal dilemma was resolved by Sioux enemies, who assassinated him in July, 1862. But the problem of providing his people appropriate guidance in this crucial period would torment many a Sioux leader.[42]

The Civil War delayed publication of Warren's reports. The narratives of all three expeditions appeared in a single volume in 1875. The year of publication was significant. The existence of paying quantities of gold in the Black Hills had been verified in the previous year. A year after the appearance of his reports, the climactic battles of the Sioux war would be fought. The slim volume carried a dual message to those eager to seek their fortunes in the Sioux homeland. While it contained the maps and data that travelers to the region so badly needed, it also delineated the potential consequences for those willing to take the risks. Captain Humphreys's introduction to Warren's 1857 report, pertinent when written in 1858, was even more meaningful in 1875: Warren's narrative, Humphreys wrote, gave "the objections urged by the Dakotas against the passage . . . through the territory. This may prove valuable to any white man that may travel there."[43]

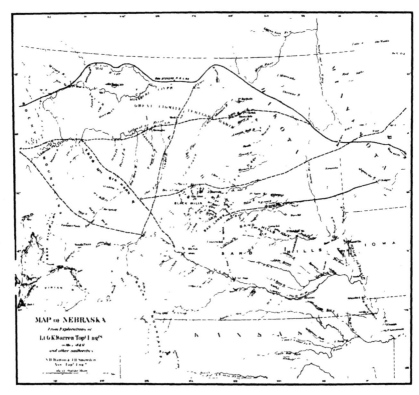

Warren's map of the northern plains. *National Archives.*

At the end of 1858, with the map just published and three western explorations under his belt, Warren could have rested on his well-earned laurels. As he told his father, he had "every reason to believe I have gained for myself a good reputation as a Topographical Engineer."[44] But the frontier had found its way into Warren's blood. His discussions with Jim Bridger and other mountainmen whetted his appetite for the Yellowstone country, the fabulous wonderland of bubbling mud and hot water spouts first visited by John Colter after he left the Lewis and Clark expedition for the life of a trapper in the northern Rockies. After Colter, most of the stories about the strange region came from Bridger. Few people accepted his tales: either the Yellowstone was the most bizarre place in the country or—as many people believed—Bridger was the nation's biggest liar. Warren wanted to see for himself. He presented Captain Humphreys with a detailed proposal for the exploration, which Warren hoped might reveal connections between Utah and navigable portions of the upper Missouri. Bridger, Warren knew, would accompany any party into the area to regain his reputation for truth. Humphreys recommended approval of the project. With his experience and ability, Warren was the right man to fill this blank space on the map.[45]

Yet when the Yellowstone expedition set out in the spring of 1859, Warren was not at its head. Earlier in the year, his father died. Then Warren accepted a position as assistant professor of mathematics at West Point to be near his younger brothers and sisters at the family home in Cold Springs.[46]

While Warren packed his books and papers for the trip to New York, Captain William F. Raynolds left Fort Pierre for the Yellowstone. This was his first expedition, but several members of his party were veterans. Along with topographers Snowden and Hutton and geologist Hayden was Bridger, still eager for the opportunity to silence skeptics.[47]

On the way westward over the high plains and along the western slopes of the Big Horns to the Oregon Trail on the Sweetwater, Raynolds took careful note of the herds of buffalo. The wholesale slaughter of the females for their hides distressed him. Ten years earlier, Captain Stansbury had placed the bison on his personal list of endangered species. Raynolds agreed: "I think it is more than probable that another generation will witness almost the entire extinction of this noble animal." Another member of Raynolds's party, an obvious tenderfoot, reacted differently to the shaggy beasts. Startled by three bulls charging at the party, the soldier dropped his rifle in terror and exclaimed, "Elephants! Elephants! My God! I did not know there were elephants in this country!"[48]

While the affair of the elephants and a feud with a grizzly bear for control of a plum patch entertained Raynolds, he was not amused by his conference with the Crow Indians at Fort Sarpy. The alleged theft of a Crow chief's horse by Blackfeet disrupted the meeting, and the Crows refused to continue the discussion until the animal was recovered. They finally found the horse browsing in a nearby wood. Raynolds cooled his heels until the Indians returned for what the topog called "the discussion of such secondary questions as the relations of the Crows and the President."[49]

Crow manners had irritated Raynolds, but he confronted a much greater problem as the party settled into winter quarters at an abandoned Mormon village near the Sweetwater and the Upper Platte Indian Agency. Here the soldiers of the escort became uncontrollably drunk and deserted. So the greatly reduced exploring party spent the winter unprotected.

For the men snowbound with the devoutly religious Raynolds, the winter was an involuntary religious retreat. Raynolds held services every Sunday and even during the week, reading scripture and sermonizing to the unkempt and uninterested audience. Even in the summer months he consistently halted operations for Sabbath observances. On one occasion, when the urgent need to reach a prearranged rendezvous with Lieutenant Henry Maynadier forced him to march on Sunday, at least one soldier became confused and refused to believe it was Sunday. "Don't you know," he told another, "the Captain never moves on Sunday!"[50]

When spring came, Bridger thought he finally had his chance to lead a government explorer to the Yellowstone and prove the existence of the geysers and other strange phenomena. But he and Raynolds were thwarted at every turn by the terrain and the deep snows. They went up the Wind River to its headwaters, only to confront a huge basaltic ridge between them and the sources of the Yellowstone. Although Bridger claimed "a bird can't fly over that without taking a supply of grub along," Raynolds persisted.[51] Finally, Raynolds led the party southwestward around the fabled region. With Grand Teton visible on their right, they tried every possible path north to the Yellowstone. Unable to penetrate any of the snow-covered approaches, Raynolds finally conceded defeat and circled the region by way of Jackson's Hole, Teton Pass, and Pierre's Hole. On 12 July 1860, the party arrived at the Great Falls of the Missouri, after passing almost completely around their objective.

Although Raynolds and Bridger were sorely disappointed, some writers have suggested that their failure was a happy one. The Engineer and historian Hiram Chittenden believed "the Yellowstone wonderland was spared the misfortune of being discovered at so early a day—a fact quite as fortunate as any in its history."[52] A more recent student of the area, David J. Saylor, has credited Raynolds with discouraging railroad construction across the continental divide to Jackson's Hole and the Yellowstone. Thus, he unwittingly contributed to later efforts by conservationists to protect the natural grandeur.[53]

In addition to this accidental achievement, Raynolds made substantial contributions to knowledge of the area. Prior to his reconnaissance, so little accurate information was available that Warren had wisely left the Upper Yellowstone blank on his map, rather than fill it with conjecture. Raynolds brought back data with which some of the unknown area could be depicted. His maps, which placed Bridger's knowledge of the mountains on the record, became basic guides for the Army during the Sioux wars of the mid–1870's.[54] The heart of the wonderland, at the grand canyon of the Yellowstone, and the bubbling mudpots, would remain a blank space until after the Civil War, when other Engineers completed the exploration of the region.[55]

Raynolds's expedition ended an era in western exploration. Since Frémont's first reconnaissance in 1842, officers of the Topographical Engineers had probed, surveyed, and mapped portions of the trans-Mississippi West. Raynolds was the last topog to lead an exploring party: during the Civil War his corps again merged with the Corps of Engineers, and the Topographical Bureau was abolished.[56] In the post-Civil War West, the Army and the Corps of Engineers would continue to play an important role. But the topogs were no more.

Notes

1. Gouverneur K. Warren to Sylvanus Warren, 6 October 1851, Warren Papers, New York State Library, Albany.
2. William A. Ganoe, "Gouverneur K. Warren," *Dictionary of American Biography*, X (New York: Charles Scribner's Sons, 1964), pp. 473-74; Roald Tweet, *A History of the Rock Island District Corps of Engineers* (Rock Island: U. S. Army Engineer District, 1975), p. 25; Emerson G. Taylor, *Gouverneur Kemble Warren, The Life and Letters of an American Soldier 1830-1882* (Boston: Houghton Mifflin, 1932), pp. 8-10.
3. Fred B. Hackett, Calendar for Oglala Sioux Names for Years from A. D. 1759 to A. D. 1908, Wyoming State Archives and Historical Department; Hyde, *Spotted Tail's Folk*, pp. 50-54; Robert M. Utley, *Frontiersmen In Blue, The United States Army and the Indian 1848-1865* (New York: Macmillan, 1967), pp. 114-15.
4. Goetzmann, *Army Exploration*, pp. 406-07; Captain George Thom to Major William H. Emory, 6 March 1855, William H. Emory Papers, Yale University.
5. Gouverneur K. Warren, Journal While on Sioux Expedition in 1855, Warren Papers.
6. Warren, Journal While on Sioux Expedition in 1855.
7. Warren, *Memoir*, p. 87; Warren, Journal While on Sioux Expedition in 1855; Warren to Colonel John J. Abert, 21 March 1856, Letters Received, Topographical Bureau, National Archives, Record Group 77.
8. Warren to Colonel Abert, 9 April 1856, Letters Received, Topographical Bureau.
9. Warren to Colonel Abert, 23 August and 19 September 1855, and 28 January 1856, Letters Received, Topographical Bureau; Warren, Journal While on Sioux Expedition in 1855; Merrill J. Mattes, *The Great Platte River Road: The Covered Wagon Mainline via Fort Kearny to Fort Laramie* (Lincoln: Nebraska State Historical Society, 1969), pp. 192-93.
10. Warren to Colonel Abert, 19 September 1855, Letters Received, Topographical Bureau; Utley, *Frontiersmen in Blue*, p. 115.
11. Utley, *Frontiersmen in Blue*, p. 115; Mattes, *The Great Platte River Road*, pp. 320-27.
12. Warren, Journal While on Sioux Expedition in 1855.
13. Mari Sandoz, *Crazy Horse, The Strange Man of the Oglalas* (Lincoln: University of Nebraska Press, 1961), p. 81.
14. Warren, Journal, 1856, Warren Papers.
15. Gouverneur K. Warren, *Preliminary Report of Explorations in Nebraska and Dakota, in the Years 1855-'56-'57* (Washington, D.C.:

Government Printing Office, 1875), pp. 14-15; W. H. Hutton, Journal for June 28-October 27, 1856, Warren Papers; Warren to William J. Warren, 24 May 1856, Warren Papers; Warren, Journal, 1856.

16. Warren, *Preliminary Report of Explorations*, p. 15; Warren to William J. Warren, 24 May 1856; Utley, *Frontiersmen in Blue*, p. 118.

17. Warren, *Memoir*, p. 90; Warren, Journal, 1856; Warren, *Preliminary Report of Explorations*, p. 15; Vincent J. Flanagan, "Gouverneur Kemble Warren, Explorer of Nebraska Territory," *Nebraska History*, 51 (Summer 1970), 183.

18. Warren, *Preliminary Report of Exploration*, p. 16.

19. Hutton, Journal for 1856.

20. Warren, *Memoir*, p. 90; Warren, *Preliminary Report of Explorations*, p. 16.

21. Warren, *Memoir*, p. 1.

22. Warren, *Memoir*, p. 1.

23. Warren, *Memoir*, pp. 92, 97-98.

24. Warren, *Memoir*, p. 92.

25. Warren, Lieut. Warren's Official Journal Commanding Explorations in Nebraska, 1857, Warren Papers.

26. Warren, *Preliminary Report on Explorations*, p. 17; J. Hudson Snowden, Journal, 27 June-14 November 1857, Warren Papers; Warren, Official Journal of 1857.

27. Warren, Official Journal of 1857.

28. Warren, Official Journal of 1857.

29. Snowden, Journal, 1857.

30. John G. Neihardt, *When the Tree Flowered, The Fictional Biography of Eagle Voice, a Sioux Indian* (Lincoln: University of Nebraska Press, 1970), p. 207; Warren, Official Journal of 1857; Warren to Sylvanus Warren, 3 September 1857, Warren Papers.

31. P. M. Engel, Report of Reconnaissance to Laramie Peak, August 22-August 27, 1857, Warren Papers.

32. Warren to Sylvanus Warren, 3 September 1857.

33. Warren, *Preliminary Report of Explorations*, p. 18; Snowden, Journal, 1857; Mari Sandoz, *Love Song to the Plains* (Lincoln: University of Nebraska Press, 1966), pp. 79-80.

34. Warren, *Preliminary Report of Explorations*, pp. 18-21; Warren, Official Journal of 1857; Snowden, Journal, 1857.

35. Snowden, Journal, 1857.

36. Snowden, Journal, 1857; Utley, *Frontiersmen in Blue*, p. 119.

37. Warren, letter draft, 27 January 1858, Warren Papers.

38. Warren, *Preliminary Report of Explorations*, pp. 51-52, 79.

39. Warren, *Preliminary Report of Explorations*, p. 53.

40. Warren, letter draft, 27 January 1858.

41. Warren, undated letter draft, Warren Papers.

42. Warren, undated letter draft; Utley, *Frontiersmen in Blue*, p. 271.

43. Quoted in Warren, *Preliminary Report of Explorations*, p. 6.
44. Warren to Sylvanus Warren, 9 December 1858, Warren Papers.
45. Audrey L. Haines, ed., *The Valley of the Upper Yellowstone: An Exploration of the Headwaters of the Yellowstone River in the Year 1869 as Recorded by Charles W. Cook, David E. Folsom, and William Peterson* (Norman: University of Oklahoma Press, 1965), p. xx; Stanley Vestal, *Jim Bridger, Mountain Man* (Lincoln: University of Nebraska Press, 1970), pp. 203, 205; Hiram M. Chittenden, *The Yellowstone National Park*, ed. by Richard A. Bartlett (Norman: University of Oklahoma Press, 1964), pp. 46, 48-49; Warren, *Preliminary Report of Explorations*, pp. 7, 10-11.
46. Warren's greatest service to the country came later, on the field of battle at Gettysburg. On 2 July 1863, the second day of the crucial battle, Warren reinforced the hill called Little Round Top just in time to fend off an attack by General John B. Hood's Confederates. The hill would have offered the enemy a commanding position on the flank of the entire Union army. Bruce Catton, *The Army of the Potomac: Glory Road* (Garden City, N. Y.: Doubleday, 1952), pp. 291-94.
47. William F. Raynolds, *Report on the Exploration of the Yellowstone River* (Washington, D.C.: Government Printing Office, 1868), p. 4; Goetzmann, *Army Exploration*, p. 418. Unless otherwise indicated, the following narrative is based on Raynolds's report. Footnotes are provided only for portions quoted in the text.
48. Stansbury, *The Valley of the Great Salt Lake*, p. 29; Raynolds, *Exploration of the Yellowstone River*, pp. 11, 34.
49. Raynolds, *Exploration of the Yellowstone River*, p. 51.
50. Raynolds, *Exploration of the Yellowstone River*, p. 67.
51. Raynolds, *Exploration of the Yellowstone River*, p. 86.
52. Chittenden, *The Yellowstone Park*, p. 55.
53. David J. Saylor, *Jackson Hole, Wyoming: In the Shadow of the Tetons* (Norman: University of Oklahoma Press, 1970), p. 99.
54. Vestal, *Jim Bridger*, pp. 205-06.
55. On post-Civil War exploration and efforts to curb vandalism in the Yellowstone, see Kenneth H. Baldwin, *Enchanted Enclosure: The Army Engineers and Yellowstone National Park, A Documentary History* (Washington, D. C.: Historical Division, Office of the Chief of Engineers, 1976).
56. Raphael P. Thian, *Legislative History of the General Staff of the Army of the United States (Its Organization, Duties, Pay, and Allowances), From 1775 to 1901* (Washington, D. C.: Government Printing Office, 1901), p. 509.

Chapter VIII

THE GREAT SURVEYS AND THE END OF AN ERA

The trans-Mississippi West to which the Engineers returned after the Civil War was vastly different from the wilderness of Major Long's time. The nation stretched westward to the Pacific, and from San Diego to Puget Sound. Towns like Omaha, Denver, Salt Lake City, and San Francisco, all destined to be large cities, grew rapidly while work parties laid track for a trans-continental railroad across the central plains, the Great Basin, and the Sierra Nevada. The clang of a hammer striking a ceremonial golden spike at Promontory, Utah, on 10 May 1869, marked the completion of the first railway to the Pacific and heralded the passing of the frontier.

The increase in western population, from about two million in 1850 to nearly seven million in 1870, brought on the climactic Indian wars of the post-Civil War decade. Tribal leaders, among them the Apache Victorio and Crazy Horse of the Oglalas, organized last, desperate efforts to preserve the autonomy and lands of their peoples. In the ranks of the blue-clad vanguard of settlement that won these wars were Engineer officers, men like Captains William J. Twining and David P. Heap, providing field commanders with maps and accompanying columns into battle.[1]

Along with the dramatic increase in western population came scientific and educational developments that defined a new era for the Engineers. Education in the sciences and engineering, once virtually the exclusive domain of the Military Academy, became available at a number of fine institutions, among them Yale's Sheffield Scientific School, the Lawrence School at Harvard, and Dartmouth's Chandler School. Frequently employing West Point graduates and curricula, these colleges made technical education available to a growing number of civilian students. The second development, the growing specialization in the sciences, was closely related to the first. Lacking a commitment to the training of military officers, the new schools could become centers for the development of such specialties as geology and paleontology. While West Pointers learned the rudiments of many fields, civilian institutions produced scientific experts and specialists.[2]

By allowing fledgling scholars to accompany western expeditions, the Engineers had encouraged the development of civilian specialists. Themselves once the students of the lone trappers and traders who first probed the mysteries of the new country, Engineer explorers soon became the teachers of others, giving young scientists like Ferdinand V. Hayden and John S. Newberry the opportunity to study frontier regions and mature in their disciplines. By the time of the great surveys—systematic postwar examinations of western resources made necessary by the rapid growth of the region—western investigation had moved through the eras of the mountainman and the officer-explorer. An era of civilian dominance was on the horizon.

Although sponsored by the Corps of Engineers, the first of the great surveys was led by a civilian, Clarence King. A masterful raconteur and close friend to Henry Adams, King graduated from the Sheffield School before gaining his first extensive field experience with Professor J. D. Whitney's California state geological survey. While working with Whitney, King conceived his plan for a federally-funded geological inquiry into the structure and mineral deposits of the country along the route of the transcontinental railroad. With the support of former Engineer explorer Colonel Robert S. Williamson, Spencer Baird, and California Senator John Conness, King went to Washington with his plan for a geological examination of a 100-mile-wide strip along the fortieth parallel line of the Union Pacific–Central Pacific railroads from eastern Wyoming to the California–Nevada border. After securing the sponsorship of Brigadier General Andrew A. Humphreys, the Chief of Engineers, King persuaded Congress to provide funds. Then he organized the expedition, selected his personnel, and set out from New York to begin work on the first of the great surveys.[3]

At the head of his United States Geological Exploration of the Fortieth Parallel, King started in 1867 on the eastern slopes of the Sierra Nevada and worked his way eastward across the Great Basin to the Wasatch range. Although his main purpose was a thorough geological analysis, he also made detailed topographical maps. Military explorers had separated knowledge of the Basin from myth and identified its features fairly well, but their maps were not sufficiently detailed to fix the locations of excavations and mineral deposits. So, while King's field parties studied the subsurface secrets of the Great Basin, they established a continuous system of triangulation across Nevada, Utah, Colorado, and Wyoming to determine trigonometrically the location of important topographical features.[4]

In the deserts and canyonlands of the Great Basin, King examined a "pretty full exposure" of the earth's crust that took in all the broad divisions of geological time. Working from the notion of zonal parallelism, first suggested by geologist William P. Blake, King observed that metal deposits occurred in parallel, longitudinal zones that followed the same patterns as the western mountain ranges. For example, a gold belt existed through the mountains that ran north from New Mexico, through Colorado, Wyoming, and Montana. Farther west, parallel to a line of mountains through western New Mexico, Utah, and western Wyoming, lay a zone of silver-bearing lodes. All the way to the Pacific-coast ranges that King had examined with Whitney, most of the parallel zones also occurred in the same geological layers. With these discoveries,

William F. Raynolds. *National Archives.*

King's survey made significant strides in the identification of mineral deposits, their location, and history.[5]

While completing his fieldwork in 1872, King began to hear rumors of spectacular deposits of precious stones in the Green River basin. The story, spread by two miners who mysteriously appeared at the office of a San Francisco banker with a bag of rubies and diamonds, was too important to ignore. If the stones actually existed in an area which King claimed to have thoroughly studied, the credibility of his survey would be destroyed. If, on the other hand, the claims amounted to a spectacular

Devil's Slide, Weber Canvon, Utah.

hoax, they had to be exposed. With the San Francisco and New York Mining Commercial Company already organized and stocks shortly to be offered to the public, King returned to northwestern Colorado to hunt for diamonds.

Back on the windswept tableland south of Fort Bridger, King and a handful of associates undertook the implausible quest. After a brief search a ruby was discovered, then several more, and finally three diamonds. With a handful of gemstones after a single day's work, all were believers. On the second day, the King party found an even larger number of diamonds and rubies, all but one just below the surface. The exceptional

One of King's survey teams at Shoshone Falls of the Snake River. *National Archives.*

gem, sitting precariously on a rock, suggested an extraordinary origin for the treasure. Before the day ended, the fraud was obvious. Amethysts, emeralds, sapphires, garnets, rubies and diamonds, an unheard-of combination in nature, were unearthed, but only where the ground had been disturbed. King hastened to San Francisco, where he revealed the swindle just in time to prevent the sale of $12 million in stock. Exposure of the diamond hoax, as great a fraud as ever concocted in the get-rich-quick West, brought him national acclaim and established the practical value of his survey.[6] "Let it not be said,"wrote the editor of a mining journal, "that geological surveys are useless. . . . This one act has certainly paid for the survey of the 40th Parallel and has brought deserved credit to Mr. King and his assistants."[7]

King's seven-volume report of his exploration was a scientific best seller. Fielding B. Meek, one of the country's leading paleontologists, wrote the section on fossils, and Robert Ridgway of the Smithsonian classified the birds with Baird's assistance. In addition, Professor Othniel C. Marsh of Yale prepared a volume on extinct toothed birds. King himself worked on two important volumes, *Systematic Geology* and *Mining Industry.* The latter, written by James D. Hague and King, quickly became very popular. Scientific critics gave it lavish praise, and the *American Journal of Science* considered it the most important contribution to the literature of mining to date. Requests for copies greatly exceeded the number printed. King's other volume, *Systematic Geology*, also received favorable notice. Henry Adams, writing in *The*

Nation, even recommended publication of an inexpensive edition for use in technological schools. The exploration of the fortieth parallel was a great success and a personal triumph for the young geologist who led it.[8]

King was still in the field when two other surveys, one under John Wesley Powell and the other under Ferdinand Hayden, began operations. At the head of the United States Geographical and Geological Survey of the Rocky Mountain Region, Powell concentrated his efforts on the lands bordering the Green and Colorado rivers, while Hayden's United States Geological and Geographical Survey of the Territories toiled in western Kansas and Colorado. Operating under the auspices of the Interior Department, these surveys shared two basic characteristics with King's Corps-sponsored enterprise: they were led and staffed by civilians and they concentrated on geology.[9]

With the proliferation of civilian surveys plainly threatening an important peacetime function of the Army, General Humphreys authorized Lieutenant George M. Wheeler to organize the United States Geographical Surveys West of the One Hundredth Meridian. An 1866 graduate of the Military Academy who married into the prestigious family of Montgomery and Preston Blair, Wheeler developed the plan for a systematic topographical survey while assigned to Brigadier General Edward O. C. Ord's Department of California. His work with Ord included a difficult reconnaissance through southeastern Nevada and western Utah, during which he made the first north-south crossing of the Great Basin since the days of the early mountainmen. Wheeler knew that western military commanders, particularly Lieutenant Colonel George Crook, who was about to begin his campaigns against the Apaches, needed detailed topographical maps. Humphreys, anxious to obtain maps that would be useful to Crook and other commanders as well as to recover for the Corps its preeminence in western exploration, agreed to Wheeler's proposal.[10]

Part precise astronomy and part detailed topography, Wheeler's first expedition in 1871 was also part showmanship. With an eye to his competition with the other surveys for popularity and funds, he asked the editors of a popular New York magazine, *Appleton's Journal,* to send a reporter to accompany him. The magazine gave the assignment to Frederick W. Loring, a 22-year-old Harvard graduate, considered "the most promising of all the young authors of America" by English novelist Charles Reade.[11] Photographer Timothy O'Sullivan, a former assistant of renowned Civil War photographer Mathew Brady and one-time employee of Clarence King, also joined Wheeler. Young Loring, the first reporter to accompany a western exploration, and the experienced O'Sullivan gave Wheeler a formidable publicity department.[12]

The 1871 effort should have provided ample grist for Wheeler's publicity mill. His party crossed the already legendary Death Valley, which was first traversed by several parties of struggling forty-niners.[13] Although three men were felled by the 120° heat, they completed the daring trek safely, and *Appleton's* readers saw the following account of the desert:

> Its heat is its greatest terror, for there is abundance of water in the canyons which open into its western side, so that thirst is to be feared more from the concealment than the scarcity of the springs. But its beauty is evil, and, though it is picturesque, it is frightful. I trust I may never have to pass through it again.[14]

The journey through Death Valley yielded important results, a map and detailed information on the location of water, but the ascent of the Colorado later in the season was superfluous. Lieutenant Ives had already

A canyon in the Uinta Mountains of Colorado.

141

Frederick W. Loring. *National Archives.*

gone up the great river to the head of navigation, and Powell had come downstream from the Green. Wheeler paid dearly for the unnecessary journey. When one of the party's three flat-bottomed boats overturned in October, at a place Wheeler named Disaster Rapids, he lost his notes and natural history collection.[15] His impetuosity and publicity-consciousness seriously diminished the results of his first season's work.

The entire party survived the hair-raising incident, but the greatest tragedy was yet to come. Accompanied by two members of the survey team, William Salmon and P. W. Hamel, journalist Loring left the party for California to report the adventures on the Colorado. He got no farther than Wickenburg, Arizona. A band of Apaches ambushed the stagecoach and killed six of the eight passengers, including Loring and his two comrades.[16]

142

The start of Lieutenant Wheeler's 1871 ascent of the Colorado.

Loring's death at the hands of the Apaches, soon followed by another defeat on the publicity front when O'Sullivan lost most of his negatives, had a great impact on Wheeler. The government's Indian policy, a benign but misguided attempt to make farmers out of warrior-hunters, seemed to Wheeler to be completely in error. Unsympathetic toward Indians or "that class of well-intentioned but illy-informed citizens who claim that the Indians are a much-abused race," he believed the Indian question in Arizona could only be settled by thoroughly defeating and subduing the Apaches.[17] His published view of Indians as irredeemable savages lent credence to unproved charges that he tortured several of them to extract information.[18] His attitude also influenced his methods. In 1875, one of his parties ransacked an Indian burial ground near Santa Barbara, California, and sent two hundred skulls east to be studied at Harvard and

143

housed in the Smithsonian. While Wheeler's attitudes and methods were far from unique, they angered many, including fellow explorer Powell who had established a rapport with the Indians of the Colorado River region.[19] Ironically, the effort to obtain favorable publicity through Loring ultimately backfired.

Although Wheeler understood from the outset that "the day of the pathfinder has sensibly ended in this country," he knew the old ground still required systematic study to blend the old routes of exploration into a coherent topographical picture.[20] And working over the terrain still involved extremely hard work. As Wheeler noted in his comments on his parties in southern Colorado and northern New Mexico, "labors in this field become exploration indeed, and hardship, fatigue, with now and then scarcity of supplies and danger from hostile Indians, falls to the lot of those who are chosen for the task. . . ."[21] In spite of the difficulties, the Wheeler parties covered much more ground than all the other surveys. They examined almost all the territory south of King's fortieth parallel

One of the Mohave Indians who accompanied Wheeler in 1871.

expedition that lay between California and the Pecos River in eastern New Mexico.

Wheeler's personnel performed this remarkable feat divided into numerous small parties. In 1874, for example, the survey worked in nine divisions, six under Army officers, two under Army surgeons, and one led by a civilian scientist. The sixteen lieutenants, usually Engineers, who assisted Wheeler between 1871 and 1879 included three who graduated at the head of their West Point classes—Eric Bergland (1869), Rogers Birnie, Jr. (1872), and Thomas W. Symons (1874).[22]

Although junior officers commanded most of the field parties, the expeditions were staffed by many illustrious men of science. Henry C. Yarrow, an Army surgeon who spent several years in the field with Wheeler as a zoologist, later became the Smithsonian's first curator of reptiles. Between 1878 and 1889 Yarrow donated his talents to the museum while pursuing his career as a military physician. Professor Edward D. Cope also aided Wheeler by collecting and evaluating minerals and fossils, while conducting one of the bitterest feuds in the annals of American science with arch-rival Othniel C. Marsh. The brilliant geologist Grove Karl Gilbert got his first western field experience with the 1871 expedition before joining the Powell survey two years later.[23]

During his first years in the field, Wheeler gradually refined his techniques and procedures. In 1873 the three divisions of his survey, led by Wheeler and Engineer Lieutenants William Marshall and Richard L. Hoxie, examined 72,500 square miles of terrain in four states and territories. Hoxie, operating in the Utah canyonlands, took readings at nearly 1,500 topographical and triangulation stations and measured over one thousand miles of meander lines. Each night he and topographer Gilbert Thompson, once an enlisted soldier in the Engineer Battalion, computed the latitude of their position, drew their meander-line profiles of the terrain, and recorded principal topographic features. While Hoxie mapped nearly 6,000 square miles of what he called "a very difficult mountain and canyon country," Wheeler in Arizona and New Mexico and Marshall in Colorado performed similar duties.[24]

While in South Park west of the Front range of the Colorado Rockies, Marshall confronted a strange and unexpected problem. About the same time that he entered the area, one of the Hayden parties arrived. Eventually four of Hayden's five field divisions came on the scene. Leaders of both surveys claimed the right to examine the park, and neither side relented. So both set up their instruments on the same mountains and went about their redundant business.[25] When this ridiculous state of affairs came to the attention of Congress, an investigation became inevitable.

While the congressional investigation of 1874 settled nothing, it revealed a great deal. Hayden, disliked by even his former teacher Newberry as "so much a fraud that he has lost the sympathy and respect of the scientific men of the country,"[26] threatened to use the influence he had

145

The Grand Canyon of the Colorado, near Paria Creek, looking east.

carefully built by hiring the relatives of political patrons and distributing collections of western photographs to destroy Wheeler.[27] Powell assailed Wheeler before the House Committee on Public Lands, selecting the worst example of the lieutenant's work to assert that all his maps were worthless for geologists. King, beholden to the Corps for sponsoring his survey, kept his own counsel, but the rest of the civilian scientific community, with much to gain from the elimination of military competition, supported Hayden and Powell. Nearly all of the scientists were convinced that civilian schools had surpassed the Military Academy in training personnel for precise surveys. Those who had worked for the Army also resented the constraints of military supervision, particularly

A sacred dance at the Zuni Pueblo, New Mexico, 1878.

the requirements for frequent reports. Although the investigation began as an inquiry into duplication and waste, the issue crystallized as civilian versus military control of western exploration. Reprieved only by the backing of President Grant, Wheeler knew his survey's days were numbered.[28]

The consolidation issue remained unresolved while Wheeler continued his fieldwork. In the mid-1870's, his parties examined contiguous north-south strips, carefully recording their topographical findings. Divisions of the survey ranged far and wide, from the Sangre de Cristo range in southern Colorado in 1875, to Lake Tahoe, one of the crowning beauties of the Sierra, in 1876.[29] In 1877 and 1878 parties worked in six different states and territories, integrating their work with surveys performed in earlier years. Aware all the while that his survey was in danger of termination, Wheeler hoped to present the War Department "at as early a date as possible, a complete map of the entire territory."[30]

When Wheeler returned to the field, he also renewed his public relations efforts. Once again he had his reporter, this time William H. Rideing, the author of fifteen books and a contributor to the New York *Times*, *Appleton's*, and *Harper's*.[31] In 1875, the city-bred journalist, attired in a dapper hunting suit, joined the flannel- and buckskin-clad surveyors in Colorado. Although he stayed with Wheeler for two seasons, he never seemed comfortable in the wilderness. Campfires, he once wrote, only reminded him that his back was cold. And the Arizona desert, warm enough to be sure, had its own nuisances, mainly "a thousand crawling things"—rattlesnakes, centipedes, beetles, and lizards.[32] Through it all, Rideing never lost his sense of humor. Staring at a dinner served hastily in a Rocky Mountain cloudburst, he found "a geological sort of mess," which he described with the precision of a Newberry or King:

> The upper crust consisted of dried apples, and beneath this was a stratum of baked beans, in which a small fossilized tree in the shape of a pickled cauliflower was imbedded. Exploring further, and with increasing interest, I unearthed some doughy bread permeated with bacon grease, and a teaspoonful of sugar evidently deposited in the wrong place during the confusion of the moment.[33]

While the leaders of all four surveys competed for public funds and published all manner of puffery, from lavishly illustrated books to stereopticon slides, Congress referred the consolidation question to the National Academy of Sciences. The result was a foregone conclusion. The Academy represented the community of civilian professional scientists and could be expected to support its constituents.[34]

The death of Joseph Henry, secretary of the Smithsonian and president of the academy, in the spring of 1878, virtually insured a decision against the Engineers. While president of the academy, Henry had advocated a coordinated cooperative effort by the competing surveys and the agencies they represented. He had encouraged the academy to study the matter and recommend a solution that might include all the competitors in any consolidation. When Henry died, Professor Marsh became interim president and selected the committee to review the matter for Congress. Marsh's well-known views, shaped by his conviction that military control was restrictive, were also colored by his friendship with Powell and his hostility toward Wheeler's former employee, Professor Cope. Although several members of the academy, including military officers like General Humphreys, supported continued Engineer involvement, Marsh selected the investigating committee with such care that this view went unrepresented.[35]

As expected, the academy report recommended consolidation of the surveys under civilian leadership. The academy proposed establishment of the United States Geological Survey to study the geological structure and economic resources of the public domain. In 1879, after Congress agreed and appropriated funds for the new agency, Clarence King received the appointment as the survey's first director. With a few exceptions, notably Alaskan exploration, the era of the Engineer-explorer was over.[36]

Although the Wheeler survey was cut short, its results were impressive. Between 1871 and 1879 the various field parties examined and mapped nearly one-fourth of the region west of the one-hundredth meridian. Concentrating on the Southwest, Wheeler studied over two hundred mining districts and 143 mountain ranges. His collectors also accumulated over 61,000 botanical, zoological, geological, and ethnological specimens, many of which were new to science. He contributed most of these to the Smithsonian. These achievements support his own overall assessment of his work as "a permanent contribution to the geography, topography, and natural history of 359,065 square miles of the western portion of the United States."[37]

There are few man-made monuments to the men who wore the gold braid of topogs or the black trim of Engineers on their uniforms. A stone marker commemorates the massacre of Captain Gunnison and several of his assistants in the summer of 1853. But the names of many of the soldier-explorers remain on the land they helped open, not on monuments. For example, at least six mountains, Whipple, Sitgreaves, and Graham in Arizona; Long's Peak in Colorado; Emory Peak in the Big Bend country of Texas; and Barlow Peak near the Yellowstone, bear the names of Engineers and topogs. Other names—among them Frémont, Gunnison, Nicollet, Raynolds, Stansbury, and Warner—on the valleys, streams, towns, and counties of the trans-Mississippi West are constant reminders of the important contributions Engineers made to western expansion and development.

Notes

1. On Engineer involvement in the Indian wars, see: George M. Wheeler, *United States Geographical Surveys*, I, pp. 629-31, 641, 648-49; Military Division of the Missouri, *Record of Engagements with Hostile Indians Within the Military Division of the Missouri, From 1868 to 1882, Lieutenant General P. H. Sheridan, Commanding* (Washington, D.C.: Government Printing Office, 1882), pp. 33, 36; Robert M. Utley, *Frontier Regulars, The United States Army and the Indian, 1866-1891* (New York: Macmillan, 1973), pp. 242-43; Donald D. Jackson, *Custer's Gold: The United States Cavalry Expedition of 1874* (New Haven: Yale University Press, 1966), pp. 2, 51-52; William S. Stanton, "Reconnaissance with Big Horn and Yellowstone Expedition," *Annual Report of the Chief of Engineers, 1876,* Appendix PP (Washington, D.C.: Government Printing Office, 1876), pp. 706-07, 710-14; Anson Mills, "The Battle of the Rosebud," *The Papers of the Order of Indian Wars,* John M. Carroll, ed. (Fort Collins: The Old Army Press, 1975), p. 7.
2. Goetzmann, *Army Exploration*, pp. 13-14; Lenore Fine, "West Point: A National College of Engineering 1802-1866," unpublished manuscript on file with the Historical Division, Office of the Chief of Engineers, pp. 29-32.
3. Thurman Wilkins, *Clarence King, A Biography* (New York: Macmillan, 1958), pp. 39, 56, 94-95, 97-98; Merrill, *First One Hundred Years of American Geology*, p. 531.
4. Clarence King, *Report of the United States Geological Exploration of the Fortieth Parallel,* Vol. I, *Systematic Geology* (Washington, D.C.: Government Printing Office, 1878), pp. 1-2, 13-14; James D. Hague with Clarence King, *Report of the United States Geological Exploration of the Fortieth Parallel,* Vol. III, *Mining Industry* (Washington, D.C.: Government Printing Office, 1877), p. 4; Wilkins, *Clarence King*, pp. 103-04.
5. King, *Systematic Geology*, p. 3; Hague with King, *Mining Industry*, pp. 5, 7.
6. Wilkins, *Clarence King*, pp. 158-72; Richard A. Bartlett, *Great Surveys of the American West* (Norman: University of Oklahoma Press, 1962), pp. 187-90.
7. Georgetown (Colorado) *Mining Review*, December 1872, quoted in Bartlett, *Great Surveys*, pp. 203-04.
8. Wilkins, *Clarence King*, pp. 154, 215; Fielding B. Meek and Robert Ridgway, *Report of the United States Geological Exploration of the Fortieth Parallel,* Vol. IV, *Paleontology and Ornithology* (Washington, D.C.: Government Printing Office, 1877), pp. 3, 308; Henry Adams, *The Education of Henry Adams,* II (New York: Time Incorporated, 1964), p. 84.

9. Bartlett, *Great Surveys*, p. 356.
10. Goetzmann, *Exploration and Empire*, pp. 399, 467; Peter L. Guth, "George Montague Wheeler, Last Army Explorer of the American West," unpublished manuscript on file with the Historical Division, Office of the Chief of Engineers, pp. 3, 6; Wheeler, *United States Geographical Surveys*, I, p. 22; Bartlett, *Great Surveys*, pp. 334, 337–38.
11. "Table-Talk," *Appleton's Journal of Science, Literature, and Art*, 6 (December 9, 1871), 666.
12. Goetzmann, *Exploration and Empire*, pp. 435, 470.
13. Carl I. Wheat, "Trailing the Forty-Niners Through Death Valley," *Sierra Club Bulletin*, 24 (June 1939), 75, 108; Frederick W. Loring, "Into The Valley of Death," *Appleton's Journal*, 6 (November 18, 1871), 574–75.
14. Loring, "Into the Valley of Death," p. 575.
15. Bartlett, *Great Surveys*, pp. 344–45; Goetzmann, *Exploration and Empire*, p. 476.
16. Bartlett, *Great Surveys*, p. 348.
17. Bartlett, *Great Surveys*, p. 348; Wheeler, *Preliminary Report Concerning Exploration and Surveys Principally in Nevada and Arizona* (Freeport, New York: Books for Libraries Press, 1970), pp. 27–28.
18. Bartlett, *Great Surveys*, pp. 343–44.
19. Wheeler, *United States Geographical Surveys*, I, p. 102.
20. Wheeler, *Explorations and Surveys in Nevada and Arizona*, p. 60.
21. George M. Wheeler, *Annual Report of Lieutenant George M. Wheeler, Corps of Engineers, Upon Explorations and Surveys West of the One Hundredth Meridian, In Nevada, Utah, Colorado, New Mexico, and Arizona, for the Fiscal Year Ending June 20, 1873*, 42d Cong., 2d sess., House of Representatives Executive Document 1, pt. 2, Vol. II, p. 125.
22. Guth, "George Montague Wheeler," p. 20; Bartlett, *Great Surveys*, p. 353. The other thirteen officers were Stanhope E. Blunt, Eugene Griffin, Richard L. Hoxie, Daniel W. Lockwood, Henry H. Ludlow, David A. Lyle, Montgomery M. Macomb, Phillip M. Price, Benjamin H. Randolph, Andrew H. Russell, Samuel E. Tillman, Charles W. Whipple, and Willard Young. Bartlett, *Great Surveys*, p. 353.
23. Henry C. Yarrow, Memorandum, 1 March 1887, Yarrow Papers, Smithsonian Institution Archives; Wheeler, *United States Geographical Surveys*, I, pp. 57, 84; Wheeler, *Annual Report for the Fiscal Year Ending June 30, 1875*, 44th Cong., 1st sess., House of Representatives Executive Document 1, pt. 2, Vol. II, p. 923; Bartlett, *Great Surveys*, p. 315.
24. Wheeler, *United States Geographical Surveys*, I, p. 58; Wheeler, *Annual Report of Lieutenant George M. Wheeler, Corps of*

Engineers, for the Fiscal Year Ending June 30, 1874, 43d Cong., 2d sess., House of Representatives Executive Document 1, pt. 2, Vol. II, pp. 480-82.

25. Goetzmann, *Exploration and Empire*, p. 468; Wilkins, *Clarence King*, p. 232; Bartlett, *Great Surveys*, p. 310.
26. Quoted in Wilkins, *Clarence King*, p. 234.
27. Wilkins, *Clarence King*, p. 234; Goetzmann, *Exploration and Empire*, p. 479.
28. Goetzmann, *Exploration and Empire*, pp. 479-81; Bartlett, *Great Surveys*, pp. 310, 354-55; Guth, "George Montague Wheeler," pp. 13-15.
29. Wheeler, *Annual Report, 1875*, pp. 935-36; Wheeler, *United States Geographical Surveys*, I, p. 103.
30. Wheeler, *Annual Report of Lieutenant George M. Wheeler, Corps of Engineers, for the Fiscal Year Ending June 30, 1878*, 45th Cong., 3d sess., House of Representatives Executive Document 1, pt. 2, Vol. II, p. 1423.
31. Bartlett, *Great Surveys*, p. 356.
32. William H. Rideing, *A-Saddle in the Wild West* (London: J. C. Nimmo and Bain, 1879), pp. 95-98; Bartlett, *Great Surveys*, p. 362.
33. Rideing, *A-Saddle in the Wild West*, p. 115.
34. Guth, "George Montague Wheeler," p. 49; Dupree, *Science in the Federal Government*, p. 479; Howard D. Kramer, "The Scientist in the West," *Pacific Historical Review*, 12 (September 1943), 239.
35. Wilkins, *Clarence King*, pp. 230-31; Dupree, *Science in the Federal Government*, p. 205; Guth, "George Montague Wheeler," p. 49.
36. Dupree, *Science in the Federal Government*, pp. 207, 209; Wilkins, *Clarence King*, pp. 232-33; Goetzmann, *Exploration and Empire*, p. 488.
37. Bartlett, *Great Surveys*, p. 367; Wheeler, *United States Geographical Surveys*, I, p. 146.

Note on Sources

The reports of individual expeditions provided the basic source material for this study. Most of these narratives were published as government documents, which sit obscure and covered with dust in the stacks of major libraries. Some have been rescued from such concealment in modern, annotated editions. A few of the reports exist only in manuscript form and are contained in Record Group 77 at the National Archives, a valuable collection of correspondence and documents relating to the Corps. Also important is the private correspondence of participants in explorations, such as the papers of William H. Emory at Yale University.

In addition to these primary sources, there is a large body of literature on the explorers, mountainmen, and nineteenth century science. William H. Goetzmann's *Army Exploration in the American West, 1803-1863*, and *Exploration and Empire, the Explorer and the Scientist in the Winning of the American West* are invaluable. Also very useful is W. Turrentine Jackson's *Wagon Roads West: A Study of Federal Road Surveys and Construction in the Trans-Mississippi West, 1846-1869*. Readers who wish to read further on the role of the Corps in western expansion should consult these books and the footnotes at the end of the chapters of this narrative.

Index

159

CPSIA information can be obtained at www.ICGtesting.com
Printed in the USA
BVOW05s1727150514

353491BV00003B/739/P